# SUCCESSION THINKING

## Bill Withers

To Deb, for your contribution and support
in our entrepreneurial partnership.

Love
Bill

# ABOUT BILL WITHERS

Bill Withers, a seasoned SME Owner-Leader from 1987 to 2023, embarked on a transformative 36-year journey that shaped his profound understanding of succession thinking. Throughout this period, he led three distinct SMEs, each with its unique visions and purposes. Bill's ventures weren't just businesses; they were integral in the discovery and funding of their successors, revealing the enduring nature of value creation. It was within the intricate dynamics of leadership and decision-making that he recognised the essence of long-term success, emphasising the vital role of culture and people in this equation.

Starting his professional life as a technician, Bill found his passion as a computer programmer, a role that allowed him to invent solutions and unravel complicated problems. Over 15 years, he adeptly transitioned into various roles, including owner, director, organisation leader, and team leader. The founding of acQuire in 1996 marked a pivotal moment in his career, where he not only honed his skills as a leader and owner/director but also uncovered the power of role clarity and seamless role handovers. This revelation became the foundation of his succession thinking, weaving together the threads of experience and insight.

Driven by an unwavering passion for equality of opportunity and the vision of a stable society, Bill Withers passionately advocated for SMEs as the cornerstone of a resilient economy. His belief in succession thinking as a means to enhance SME stewardship and redirect capital towards these vital economic contributors shaped his mission. In his perspective, a network of 100,000 strong SMEs stood as a testament to antifragility, countering the vulnerabilities of 'too big to fail' corporations. SMEs, in Bill's eyes, represented the essence of humanity in business, fostering innovation even in the face of scarce resources.

For more information about his journey, please visit
www.linkedin.com/in/bill-withers/

# ACKNOWLEDGEMENTS

I would like to acknowledge all the people who were stakeholders of Metech, acQuire and ADAPT. I had the good fortune to work with many wonderful people. Many of them contributed in some way to the concepts discussed in this book.

I would also like to thank the people who supported the production of the book. I had a lot to learn and your feedback was very valuable.

Book Coach: Kath Walters
Publishing Partner: Publish Central (Michael Hanrahan and Anna Clemann)
Story Telling: Mitchell Withers

And thanks also to my first readers:

| | |
|---|---|
| Mary Gentile | Kane Leersen |
| Sue Male | Doug Bester |
| Hamish Tedesci | Shane Addis |
| Gillian Bester | Wayne French |
| Steve Tapley | Tim Dobush |
| Gabe Enslin | Dean Gilkinson |
| Dave Stephen | Dave Andrew |
| Suzie McGrechan | Suzanne Oxford |
| Zoe Finlay-Jones | Mark Runnalls |
| Tadhg MacArthy | |

First published in 2023 by Bill Withers

A catalogue entry for this book is available from the National Library of Australia.

ISBN: 978-1-923007-51-2

Printed in Australia
Book production and text design by Publish Central
Cover design by Pipeline Design.
Cover graphic by New World Order.

The paper this book is printed on is certified as environmentally friendly.

**Disclaimer**
The material in this publication is of the nature of general comment only, and does
not represent professional advice. It is not intended to provide specific guidance
for particular circumstances and it should not be relied on as the basis for any
decision to take action or not take action on any matter which it covers. Readers
should obtain professional advice where appropriate, before making any such
decision. To the maximum extent permitted by law, the author and publisher disclaim
all responsibility and liability to any person, arising directly or indirectly from any
person taking or not taking action based on the information in this publication.

# CONTENTS

# INTRODUCTION

Let me share a personal story about how I learned about the importance of succession thinking.

In mid 2008 the Global Financial Crisis was in full swing. Even
though our business had done very well in the preceding five years,
the challenges thrown up by this economic event were starting to
give me some concerns.

Our business – Acquire Technology Solutions (acQuire) – is a
software company in the field of geoscientific information management. My role as the Owner-Leader of acQuire is very demanding.
acQuire is a small to medium enterprise (SME) with offices in Perth,
Brisbane, Calgary and Santiago. At that time, we were growing at
around 50% per annum and our products were in high demand.
We had around 80 people in the business; in 2003 we had 15 people
and no international offices. Although we'd had this strong recent
growth, the Global Financial Crisis was starting to impact our
pipeline.

Then one afternoon in mid-July, I was in my office chatting
with Craig about a new product. We were debating ideas about
its design. Lauren, our receptionist, put a call through from my

1

wife, Debbie. Before she spoke a word I heard her choke back tears. I asked where she was and what was wrong. She struggled to say, 'Sammy doesn't know who I am.' Sammy is our son, who was 11 at the time. He was in an ambulance on the way to the emergency department.

This was his first epileptic seizure.

Four months prior to this, Deb had been diagnosed with lupus. Although it is unusual for lupus to be life threatening, her father died of nephritis (a lupus complication of the kidney). So this gave us great cause for concern.

As the health of family members deteriorated around me and the demands of the GFC increased, my anxiety rose significantly. I increasingly struggled to reconcile supporting my family with dealing with the demands of my business. I called a meeting with the owners of acQuire – the three fellow shareholders of the company – and asked, 'What do we do now? I might have to become a primary carer.'

Life happened to me with Debbie's and Sam's diagnoses, and I had several big lessons:

- **Life events can affect you at any time**, so make your business resilient and able to deal with them. Don't put it off to the future. Do it *now*.
- **I was too central to all that was going on**. The impact on the business was going to be significant because I had too many core roles.
- **Selling a business while in a reactive state is not wise.** As owners, we discussed the idea of selling. However, I was not at my best to contribute to the big thinking required. I needed to do this thinking when things were going well.

We made it through these challenging times, and I continued as an Owner-Leader of acQuire. However, in the subsequent years we began implementing strategies that would drive us to be more resilient while meeting the aspirations of the owners.

## The origins of succession thinking

These events of 2008 were a catalyst for many of the ideas in this book. However, my family and my entrepreneurial experiences prior to 2008 also contributed significantly to succession thinking.

### Family influences

My parents had a big impact on how I developed my business mindset. They were very entrepreneurial. In 1964, my parents – with another family – drove from Sydney to Kununurra, Western Australia. Their vehicle was a double-decker bus.[1] They tackled the 4000 kilometres of unsealed roads with three kids. When they arrived in Kununurra they founded the first general store. They subsequently built a service station, a gift shop, a diamond jeweller and a mango plantation.

Kununurra was a young remote town with a population of 300. There was a great sense of community where people helped each other out. This combination of small business and the importance of community had a big impact on me. My environment and my family's influence drove my values of 'a fair go' and 'have a go'. Unfortunately, today these terms have been hijacked by politicians. However, the idea of being accountable while looking out for others appealed to me.

---

1    www.youtube.com/watch?v=w_TdRLw31sE.

## Entrepreneurial influences

After completing my degree at the Western Australian Institute of Technology, I joined a business called Metech – Mine Evaluation Technologies – as the first employee in 1984. Metech was founded by Charlie Bass as a consulting service to conduct resource definition and mine planning. I was employed as a technical software engineer to develop solutions.

In 1988, I became an owner and leader of Metech. We changed the direction of the business in the following years to become a software and services company. We developed a variety of software systems across the mining value chain, such as 3D geological solid modelling and stockpile modelling. In doing so we discovered a significant underserved need in the way geoscientific observations and measurements were being managed. This discovery led to the founding of acQuire.

We – Andy Shoemack and I – founded acQuire in 1996, and for the next 10 years had two businesses that were complementary but distinctly different. Metech had a partner in Arizona called Mintec. We had an agreement to develop products and services around their Mindsight product, and they could develop solutions and services around our acQuire product.

In 2006, Andy and I mutually agreed to transition out of our other businesses. This decision was driven by many factors, not least of which was the extensive growth of acQuire.

As stated previously, life and economic events of 2008 had a big impact on me and were a catalyst for new ideas. These new ideas were directed at how to run a global SME and make it more resilient. In 2009 I handed over all operation roles, so I had time to do the research on how we are going to run our business and solve the resilience challenge. We established a team called 'Commercial Research & Development' to study this problem. Given I had no daily demands from operations I could immerse myself in this. My personal purpose had evolved: I no longer wanted to solve geoscience data challenges – I wanted to focus on how to build and lead a global SME.

Between 2009 and 2014 we did a lot of work on how to build our global SME. We committed to leadership development, cultural leadership and systemising our business. Through these initiatives I was able to hand over being an organisation leader and move on to the founding of ADAPT by Design. We now had a holding company called Metech Holdings which had two subsidiaries: acQuire and ADAPT. My new roles were to be Chairman of the Metech Holdings Board and the Founding Leader of ADAPT.

ADAPT was created to continue the work I had started at acQuire. I wanted to build a solution to help other SME Owner-Leaders build their business so resilience is wired in. I recognised there was no SME-specific leadership system dealing with building a business that can deliver sustained results and navigate uncertainty, which can be associated with both life and economic events.

## Who is this book for?

My motivation in writing this book is to support people who make the big decision to form their own business and take the associated financial and life risks. I care about this because I often felt lonely in my businesses, and I know this is very common for SME leaders. Succession thinking has been founded to solve the needs of Owner-Leaders of an SME, not publicly listed corporations or any other organisation type.

Throughout the book I will make references to the Australian economy. This is simply expedience and access to knowledge. Where possible I will reference other countries. The intention is that this book is for SME owners in all parts of the world. There are many countries' economies underwritten by the performance of their SME sector.

The United Nations and many countries define an SME as an enterprise employing up to 249 persons. My definition of an SME is where there is a big overlap between ownership and leadership. The people working in the business are also the owners of the business. These people must run their business in a way acceptable to the jurisdiction in which they operate. Through their ownership they can make decisions about the vision for their business. They can then implement strategies and make choices to deliver that vision. The sum of all of these decisions can be referred to as 'decision rights'. The people with these decision rights will be called Owner-Leaders.

I am also motivated to see SMEs become a more visible part of our national and global economy, and to get more support. I believe there will be many benefits to the Owner-Leaders and society if SMEs are built with succession thinking at their core. According to the Australian Bureau of Statistics, in August 2021 there were 7.8 million employed persons in small and medium enterprises in Australia. This accounts for approximately 66% of total employment in Australia. If you can be part of a more resilient economy led by SMEs, there would be many benefits. Legislators, educators and financial institutions may see the possibilities of being more supportive to this type of economic contributor.

Succession thinking is an approach for how to build an SME. It can be effectively applied to SMEs at any stage from startup to mature. The key is the mindset of the SME Owner-Leader, not the stage of the business.

When people hear the term 'succession' they tend to think it is something that happens at the end; the end of a career, or the end of ownership of a business. But succession thinking is centred on the idea that a business founded on the basis of distributing leadership and accountability will get many benefits. An SME can deliver for the long term if the people who make up that business are truly engaged. Therefore, succession thinking drives trust and clarity of accountability as core building blocks of a business.

Succession thinking will resonate with you if you acknowledge the primacy of people and clarity of accountability as central to good business practice. I acknowledge that this is difficult to do when you have the daily demands of business. However, for those with the aligned mindset, I believe you can accelerate your leadership capability and get the subsequent benefits.

I recommend that you be patient as you read this book. The solutions will unfold. I often recommend that Owner-Leaders 'park the car' to work on their business. The expression comes from working with people who will decelerate to 80 km/h but not actually come to a halt and be fully present.

My recommendation for reading this book is to park the car.

## Defining succession thinking

Succession thinking is a method for how SME Owner-Leaders steward their business. This includes decision making as owners, directors and leaders, and how you design and build your business.

I have chosen the term 'stewardship' to describe the leadership of SMEs. Organisational stewardship means seeing a key accountability of your own role is that the business thrives beyond your tenure.

You acknowledge that you are accountable to supporting the success of your successors. Within an organisation, stewardship encourages a more cooperative environment focused on group success. This makes sense because it will most likely lead to better outcomes for you as the owner.

An alternative term is 'SME governance'. Governance encompasses the system by which an organisation is controlled and operates, and the mechanisms by which it and its people are held to account. Ethics, risk management, compliance and administration are key elements of governance. But I have chosen SME stewardship over SME governance because it is more suitable for the principles of succession thinking.

If you, as an SME owner, adopt a stewardship mindset, you'll be more successful in the long term. You need to hand the business over to others, so a cooperative environment is essential. The words 'control' and 'compliance' do not sit well with building adaptive organisations.

I discovered succession thinking while building Metech, acQuire and ADAPT. Many advisers I engaged referenced governance from publicly listed corporations, but we, as SME Owner-Leaders, need a stewardship system specifically designed for our needs. An approach that harnesses the SME advantages of being small and agile, and where incentives align.

Stewardship is about how you make decisions in your business. These decisions will be driven by your worldview and your mindset. You, as an Owner-Leader of an SME, have rights that corporate boards and executives don't have – or rarely, anyway. Your business is a system that human beings can get their head around. Although complex, your business is at the simple end of the scale. This gives you great opportunities to design your business in an entirely different way.

## The core message of this book

Your business may be financially successful, but you are probably still central to too many decisions. Feelings of being stuck, overwhelmed or lonely are common. Succession thinking is an SME business-building approach to help you build a resilient business – a business that can be successful beyond you. A business that can create sustained value and deliver long-term success. The application of succession thinking can deliver this while also increasing the value of your business. And it is an approach to building your SME where you don't lose your entrepreneurial roots.

*Your business may be financially successful, but you are probably still central to too many decisions.*

When you started your business, your core motivations may have been solving a specific problem and being your own boss. Or it may have been to develop new wealth-creation opportunities. Whatever your founding story, the journey develops and your motivations change. What do you now want your business to deliver and for whom?

This book provides direction to support you as an Owner-Leader to be clear about what you want and how to deliver it. It supports you in building a stewardship system that is specifically designed for you as an Owner-Leader of an SME. Your business will be driven by investing in people because it is essential for good business. You can design your business to challenge power hierarchies and ideas that undermine sustained success. Your business can develop leaders who serve the total business and know they're accountable for the success of their successor. Your financial success will be an outcome of stewardship excellence.

## Terminology

I have included a glossary at the end of the book. Part A of this glossary is terms that are commonly used but I have clarified their meaning for their use in this book. Part B is for terms I have introduced as part of succession thinking. In the glossary I explain the term and why I introduced this term.

## What's coming up?

So, here's what's in store for you:

- **Chapter 1: SME opportunities and challenges.** This is an exploration of the challenges that are common to most SME Owner-Leaders. You, as an Owner-Leader, will probably identify with most of these. I also introduce the idea of harnessing the advantages of your SME. In the past, many thought that 'big is best'. But the evidence is mounting that small is beautiful because we need to be agile in an ever-changing world.
- **Chapter 2: Introducing succession thinking.** Succession *thinking* is not succession *planning*. The distinction is important because it helps to underscore why succession thinking is a way of building as well as handing over a business. I introduce the five principles and how, with their application, you can build your Business Way. An important part of this chapter is understanding that trust is the essential fuel of succession thinking.

- **Chapter 3: Principle one: Seek role clarity.** To become a succession thinker, you need to acknowledge you have different roles. The lack of visibility of these roles can create confusion for all, including you. By acknowledging this, you can apply the principle of role clarity across your business. The clarity between owner, director and organisation leader is the starting point.

- **Chapter 4: Principle two: Build your owners' vision.** When there are multiple owners, your integrated owners' vision is the source of all decision making. This is the combination of the star on the horizon merged with the guardrails of your business. The star is where you want to head, and the guardrails help you get there. The guardrails will remain in place as you hand over decision rights.

- **Chapter 5: Principle three: Build leadership beyond you.** The central measure of success for you as a succession thinker is when you've handed over roles you no longer want to do. This will not happen without understanding how leadership works in your business. Distributing leadership to others is key to both growing a business and your succession. The problems of single leaders or leaders who don't know your Business Way are explored.

- **Chapter 6: Principle four: Build culture beyond you.** SME Owner-Leaders can harness the advantages of having a small system. You have the decision rights to define your culture. There are no constraints on how you build your culture. The only limitation is your imagination. This is the place to differentiate. To be a succession thinker, you need to attract capable and aligned people and have them contribute for the long term.

- **Chapter 7: Principle five: Build your Business Way.** Your Business Way is a set of data specifically to support SME Owner-Leaders. As a succession thinking leader, you need a place to store your

Business Way so you can provide clarity and support to current and future stakeholders. This will encourage leaders in building a resilient and adaptive business. It also supports the clarity of vision and delivers to that vision.

- **Chapter 8: Succession thinking: A case study.** At ADAPT by Design, I've gone from founder in 2014 to handing over all roles except owner and director. I share my story by explaining it through the five principles of succession thinking.

- **Chapter 9: Succession thinking, business value and capital.** You have a lot of wealth tied up in your business and future ownership. Realising the wealth by selling part or all of your business is a core part of your owner vision. You need to integrate getting what you want for the business commercially with what you want for all other stakeholders. In succession thinking, you consider all stakeholders. To make the best decision, you must be clear about your access to capital. What you do with your shareholding is the final succession challenge. In this chapter, we will explore several considerations that put you in the best position to deal with debt and equity capital decisions.

# Chapter 1
# SME OPPORTUNITIES AND CHALLENGES

## Introduction

Improving the stewardship of small to medium enterprises will provide core solutions for SME Owner-Leaders. SME owners have control of the vision of their business, and also the decision rights to implement it. As part of stewarding an SME, owners need leadership systems that support their capacity to deliver their vision.

This book supports you as an SME Owner-Leader to build a resilient SME for the long term, allowing you to:

- deliver on your aspirations
- make yourself match fit so you increase the probability of successfully navigating difficult markets, pandemics or life events
- increase the capacity for sustained value creation
- increase the value of your business for whatever the future holds regarding ownership
- embrace the essential nature of the relationships and people in your endeavour.

Resilient SMEs are tough and create sustained benefits to you and the economy. They are businesses that:

- care for their people and create higher trust environments
- are close to their community and can contribute positively
- are core to innovation and discovery of new technology and ways to solve opportunities and challenges.

You, as an SME Owner-Leader, are the silent hero of our economy. You take risks to establish a business with very limited support. Succession thinking will help you develop a new way of building a sustainable business that can thrive in the long term. As a result, you will increase the probability of meeting your goals and aspirations, while the entire economy gets the derivative social and economic benefits of your business.

Succession thinking is the product of my own SME Owner-Leader journey in three businesses over 34 years. As described in the introduction, one of my big lessons that led to succession thinking occurred in 2008 when I had the confluence of Debbie's and Sam's health events mixed with the Global Financial Crisis. We were able to navigate that period because of the support of my fellow owners. When I called a meeting with them – Andy Shoemack, Geoff Forbes and Colin Legg – and asked, 'What do we do now? I might have to become a primary carer,' they responded by saying, 'Hey, Bill, we've got your back'. My family navigated the health challenges, but those simple words from my fellow owners triggered the question: 'What if our business could have the backs of *all* its people?'

Also in 2008, we were deploying enterprise technology into large, well-funded corporations. While doing this, we observed they had a lot of dysfunction. We were building a global SME and advisers told us to use corporation logic to do so. The biggest area where we observed a big difference was in our approach to values. We paid our bills on time and cared for our suppliers. Our corporate customers would contact us in tough times and want to change our net terms from 30 days to 60 days. As well as this, they would do massive retrenchments and not care for their own people. People we had built great relationships with as customers were now out of a job. The advisers told us we could find excellence in the corporate approach, but the evidence did not stack up. We began to observe that our approach was more resilient and we were doing better at traversing the boom–bust nature of our industry. I started to recognise that corporations have drivers that make long-term thinking difficult.

The conclusion for me was that, as an SME Owner-Leader, I needed to craft a different way that would be in service of our customers, our people and the owners for the long term. We now had the founding threads that would ultimately develop into succession thinking. We were using that thinking to build the acQuire Way.

## The SME Owner-Leader challenges

As an SME Owner-Leader, you have common pains and challenges that succession thinking solves. You founded your business for many reasons. Some of these are autonomy, wanting a different method to create wealth, solving a problem in a better way and because you are skilled at what you do. These all contribute to the founding vision. You then need to decide how you're going to capitalise your venture to achieve this vision. At the start you are strategic, but as you go on this journey you may find you become swamped by the transactions of business.

The following are common outcomes:

- getting stuck – there is no succession path out
- getting burned out – a feeling like being on a hamster wheel
- wearing too many hats – all roads lead to you
- making decisions that are not in service of your vision
- making very important but detrimental decisions, such as the sale of shares to unaligned people
- not building the company you want to work in – the culture has changed
- not achieving your aspirations – you wanted more autonomy, but you are seeing less of family and friends
- having a different life trajectory to your co-founders, and their changing aspirations are challenging alignment
- having employee or customer turnover and you are not sure what to do.

An outcome you may achieve from implementing succession thinking is to set the direction to get where you want. I'm not talking about the current operational challenges of your SME. There are myriad books, advisers and solutions for that. In succession thinking, we are seeking answers to:

- Why does our business exist?
- How will we fund our business?
- How do we behave?
- Where are we going?
- What do we do – and what *don't* we do?
- How will we succeed?
- What is important now?
- Who needs to do what?

- How will we sustain our business?
  - How do we build clarity to support role handovers?
  - How do we build the 'success of my successor' mindset?
  - How do we build trust to support sustainability?

As the business grows, it is not uncommon for SME Owner-Leaders to want better returns, to grow, or to get more discretionary time. However, if you have limited answers to the questions above and you have a feeling of being overwhelmed or stuck, you need a circuit breaker.

As you build your SME, you begin to understand there is a growing accountability that is always with you. You carry the responsibilities for the customers, the employees and the existential threat of making a loss. 'I hope Mary is not under too much pressure on that project,' or, 'I'm not happy with the level of service we have given John and he's our oldest customer.' Dealing with these issues while carrying the financial burden can be overwhelming. This can push us below the line, shown in the following diagram. The above-the-line states are to be calm, creative and energetic. Below-the-line states are to be anxious, overwhelmed and tired. You solve the big challenges in business by getting above the line.

---

*As you build your SME, you begin to understand there is a growing accountability that is always with you. You carry the responsibilities for the customers, the employees and the existential threat of making a loss.*

---

When you founded your business, you were most likely at your most strategic and above the line. If you've been pushed below the line – which is not uncommon – you are not in the right headspace to

| Calm Creative Energetic | **ABOVE THE LINE** |
|---|---|
| Anxious Overwhelmed Tired | **BELOW THE LINE** |

Source: A simplified version of an open source behaviour model

make the decisions that will get you where you want to go. You need to become strategic again.

In 2003, six years after the founding of acQuire, I was still a technician in my business and all the 24 people in the business were 'led' by me. I was battling. As described in Geoffrey Moore's book *Crossing the Chasm*, we were about to grow in different regions around the world – we were about to cross the chasm. I got the idea that on Fridays at 3:00 PM we would meet in the boardroom and discuss what we were working on. By 5:00 PM I was a wreck. I dragged my schoolbag home and shared my problems with my wife, Debbie, while overindulging in a bottle of wine. I was overwhelmed. Fortunately, I had a trip to the US planned, which started with a flight from Sydney to Los Angeles. I used this 14-hour trip to concentrate on my challenges.

April 2003 was the turning point for me to move to being more proactive. I'd been there before when I founded the business. I did not know what above the line and below the line was in 2003, but I think a lot of my reactive behaviour was below the line. I needed a circuit breaker, and my trip to the US provided it.

The best time to engage with succession thinking is at the foundation of a company when you are strategic, putting the habits and practices in place early. However, you may feel, 'Everything is fine at the moment. Why do I need succession thinking?' The irony is that this is the best time to implement it. However, in 2003 and 2008, for me it took being in pain, having problems and being overwhelmed to trigger action and explore a different way. In this book I share the logic to help you dodge some of this pain and accelerate your success at achieving what you want.

## Activity: Where do you put your attention?

The following table will help you think about where you put your attention and which roles take most of your time. This set of high-level roles is common across SMEs.

| Role | Description | Attention (%) | Note |
|---|---|---|---|
| Owner | A person who has the decision rights for capital and vision. | | |
| Director | A person who has the fiduciary responsibilities of the business in the jurisdiction the business was incorporated in. | | |
| Organisation Leader | This person is responsible for:<br>• formulating and implementing business strategy<br>• ensuring the cultural health of the organisation<br>• systematising the business. | | |

| Role | Description | Attention (%) | Note |
|------|-------------|---------------|------|
| Team Leader | A person who leads an effective team to deliver defined accountabilities. | | |
| Technician | A team member who delivers on the work of the team in a specific role. | | |
| | Total | 100% | |

Use this table to determine what percentage of time you put into each of these roles throughout a work year. It is common for SME Owner-Leaders to underestimate the need for organisation leaders and effective team leaders to get what they want. This exercise helps you reflect and ponder where you put your effort and where you *want* to put your effort.

To download this activity go to: www.successionthinking.com/activities

## The SME Owner-Leader opportunities

As an Owner-Leader, you can leverage your SME advantage. I had the opportunity to get a close look at how PLCs work by implementing enterprise technology into them. I observed the differences between the characteristics of SMEs and PLCs at the same time our advisers were recommending a governance approach that seemed to be founded in the PLC way of doing things. This prompted me to conduct further research, which revealed that PLCs and private SMEs are fundamentally different types of organisations.

My intention is not to be negative about PLCs. But by emphasising this distinction we can embrace the innovation of SME stewardship not PLC governance. The following table shows the advantages available to Owner-Leaders of SMEs if they choose to harness them.

| Category | PLC | SME |
|---|---|---|
| *Vision* | In most PLCs there are a lot of owners. The vision tends to shareholder value because of the number of owners.<br><br>This is explained in greater detail in chapter 3. | You can craft a vision for your business that delivers what you want.<br><br>The small number of owners makes it possible to form an authentic vision. |
| *Stakeholders* | Given that PLCs are a primary asset class, they have a financial bias for shareholder value. | You can build your business in service of customers, people, yourself and your fellow owners by maximising stakeholder outcomes. |
| *Decision making* | Complex decision rights with a tendency to bureaucracy. | You have simple decision rights that allow you to be nimble and create innovative cultures – a more entrepreneurial approach. |
| *Design and strategy horizons* | Quarterly reporting and the financial focus reduce organic innovation. The leadership tenure model does not support succession thinking. | You are there for the life of the business. You can see through long-term strategies. You can build a handover culture and support the success of your successor. |
| *Culture* | Very few PLCs navigate downturns without major impacts on stakeholders. Reduction in the number of employees and changing terms with suppliers is common practice. | You can recognise that building teams of aligned and effective people supports long-term value creation. It takes a lot of effort to build them so you can't simply cut people that are core to success. |

In the first part of this chapter, I outlined the challenges and pains you can have as an Owner-Leader. Harnessing the SME advantages is the hope and opportunity. By harnessing these advantages, you can turn your entrepreneurial craftsmanship to the innovation of your Business Way.

Your Business Way is a set of interdependent data that defines your business and is essential for all subsequent leaders to know. Building the capability to capture your Business Way will empower you to harness the SME advantages. Think of it like a bucket of all the knowledge, wisdom and practices you think are important for all near-future leaders. These will include your owner vision, your purpose, your values, how you organise yourself and how you differentiate yourself in the market. (In chapter 2, I provide a more detailed description of your Business Way. In chapter 7, I discuss how your Business Way can be viewed as a set of data.)

A clear point of distinction for an SME is that the owners have the decision rights over the vision. Before we proceed, let's understand what I mean by vision. This definition is from the Queensland government business advice site: 'A business vision is your goal for what your business will be in the future. It will align with your business goals and aspirations.' It is the clarity of what you want your business to achieve and the philosophy for how it will achieve it. In chapter 4 this will be explored in detail. The clarity of this is essential to succession thinking and is the root of your Business Way. This vision will most likely state desires with respect to financial return. However, it can also address what you want for different stakeholders of your business.

A report written by the Commonwealth Scientific and Industrial Research Organisation (CSIRO) in 2020, called 'Small Medium

Businesses Key to Driving Growth in Australia'[2], points out how important SMEs' contribution is to research, development and innovation. One point in the article talks about the contribution of Australian SMEs to the national gross domestic product: 57%.

### 2023 SME contribution to the economy in a number of countries

| Country | % of population employed in SMEs | Contribution to GDP | Source |
|---|---|---|---|
| Australia | 66% | 57% | Australian Bureau of Statistics |
| Canada | 88.2% | 53% | https://ised-isde.canada.ca/site/sme-research-statistics/en/key-small-business-statistics/key-small-business-statistics-2022 |
| Malaysia | 66% | 38.3% | https://www.comparehero.my/sme/articles/sme-landscape-malaysia |
| UK | 61% | 51% | https://www.fsb.org.uk/uk-small-business-statistics |

If more SME Owner-Leaders harness their advantage, what could this do for getting more support, legislation and education, for instance? What could the benefits be to the greater economy? What does it mean for you if you can be part of that?

By increasing the excellence of your stewardship system in service of your own aspirations, you can also be part of the future SME economy, where SMEs have greater value, visibility and opportunity. SMEs are significant contributors to the economy and are

---

2    www.csiro.au/en/news/All/News/2022/June/Small-and-medium-businesses-key-to-driving-growth-in-Australia

key to growth and innovation. If you lean into your SME advantage, what could the future hold?

It is possible you don't feel there is any advantage to being an SME at the moment. For instance, you might compete for people and PLCs can pay more. I will expand on this in chapter 6, which is about building culture beyond you. Imagine being able to attract good people to your business because you built a way that was attractive beyond money.

### Activity: Are you harnessing the SME advantages?

Answer the following questions to reflect on the SME advantages and whether you are harnessing them.

1. Are you building your business in service of all stakeholders – your customers, your people, yourself and your fellow owners?
2. What percentage of decision rights do you have when you and your fellow Owner-Leaders get together?
3. Do you have real clarity on what your fellow owners want the business to deliver in service of their lives?
4. Does your business allow you to live the life you want, or has it taken over your life?
5. Are you an entrepreneurial or cultural leader of your business? If so, how will you hand this to others?
6. If you intend to sell your business, what have you put in place to ensure that can happen and you maximise the business value?

To download this activity go to: www.successionthinking.com/activities

## Participating in the long-term SME economy

In this section I posit what other benefits may come from building a resilient SME. Some of these points are evergreen but others are possibilities based on current trends.

As a resilient SME, you'll be more valued and visible, and will have a positive impact on the economy. By integrating solutions for your challenges with harnessing the SME advantages, you will build a resilient SME. As we will discuss in subsequent chapters, succession thinking is our approach for how you do this.

> *By integrating solutions for your challenges with harnessing the SME advantages, you will build a resilient SME.*

Resilient SMEs are built to create sustained value for the long term. They've implemented succession thinking so the business can develop from its foundations while mitigating the risk of the vision being corrupted. If our economy is built on these companies, there will be many benefits because it'll be established on a distributed network of resilient SMEs. This is a counterpoint to everything being aggregated into a small number of publicly listed companies.

Imagine a government that can now see and measure that businesses like yours are the ideal vehicle to create a resilient economy. Legislation that currently has a negative effect on SMEs could be removed. In Australia, we have the anathema to SMEs of payroll tax, one of the greatest anti-employment and anti-innovation taxes ever devised. In other jurisdictions in the world no doubt there is other legislation that does not support SMEs to flourish. This is often because a PLC and an SME are not well differentiated.

Being a resilient SME will increase the value of your business. The valuation of a business is more art than science. It's often difficult to understand, especially in early-stage PLCs or the unicorn-seeking (a company capitalised at over $1 billion) startup world. In the SME world, there are high-value businesses that at some stage may be sold. If the business is tough and not reliant on a few key people, it will be valued higher.

With succession thinking, you can go even further. You can supply more lead indicator data. This is discussed in greater detail in chapter 9. Lead indicators in business are about leadership effectiveness, culture and systemisation. An example of lead indicator data is showing the longitudinal data for the culture of your business or the detailed analysis of the effectiveness of your teams. Lag indicator data is historical financial data. This is required but alone it does not give much indication about future performance. You will get higher valuations by building a resilient SME.

When you're a part of a movement of resilient SMEs, you can mobilise new capital flows. Patient capital is capital where the investor is motivated to see the product or service come to life. A short-term return-on-investment (ROI) investor may be comfortable with a financial return where the success of the product or service is secondary. SMEs have all sorts of applications for patient capital. Unfortunately, there is limited opportunity to access this and we haven't built exchanges or banks set up to offer these solutions. When they arrive, resilient SMEs will be able to pass the prudential tests that this world will demand. Imagine being able to mobilise material amounts of our superannuation and pension funds into resilient SMEs listed on a patient capital exchange.

Imagine getting more government support because your resilient SME was recognised for making a positive contribution to the economy and society. Your resilient SME works without you, and has greater value while you have more discretionary time. You are not on the hamster wheel. Access to new capital products increases because you will pass the prudential tests. Therefore, there is great motivation to build a resilient SME, and I believe succession thinking delivers that.

In the world today, the CEO of a large, publicly listed corporation can have a lot of influence. When we built acQuire, we were an SME that became a net exporter and put our research and development centre in Perth, Australia. We did not move it overseas. However, I was a realist and I knew we were a microbe on a flea on a large dog. I recognised that a company of 120 does not have a voice and we had a profile lower than Death Valley (or the Nullarbor). Since that time, I have pondered how a collective of high-value-add SMEs could influence legislators and educators.

In the last 10 years I've met many SME owners who have built brilliant companies, and they also seem invisible to the government even though they are large contributors to GDP. Building resilient SMEs is the first step towards a bottom-up approach to influencing legislation that could have a significant impact on capital flows and negative legislation.

You may be thinking this seems a little futuristic and not tangible now. This is fair, however building a resilient business will increase value and that is here and now. Also, there is evidence of new debt funds that have been specifically designed for SMEs. Those that can show their robustness are going to have greater access to that capital at cheaper rates.

## Activity: Obtaining finance

Put yourself in the shoes of an investor or finance provider and consider what you would want to know about your business to commit funds. A few examples have been crafted below. Apply these questions to your own business and determine if you can supply answers and evidence that supports your answers.

| Question category | Questions |
|---|---|
| *Leadership* | Who currently forms and leads implementation of strategy? <br> Who leads the culture and how? <br> Who are the critical people in the business? <br> How much is centred on the owners of the business? <br> How are you going to distribute leadership to mitigate risk? <br> Who are the primary entrepreneurial leaders? |
| *People* | What is your turnover rate? <br> How engaged is the current team? <br> How effective are your teams? |
| *Customers* | What does your customer retention data look like: <br> • after 6 months? <br> • after 12 months? <br> • etc. |
| *Knowledge* | How much of the intellectual property of your business is tacit (in people's heads)? |

You may say, 'This activity is all very interesting. But I have to close this proposal on Monday or I will be under financial pressure again.' That daily demand is hard to deal with, but a theme throughout this book is that we need to change small habits to begin to build resilience into our SMEs. This exercise will help to raise awareness of where the value lies, and there is a direct connection between value and resilience.

To download this activity go to: www.successionthinking.com/activities

# Conclusion

You as an Owner-Leader of an SME are a silent hero of our economy who takes risks with limited support. The nature of your existence leads to a lonely journey with many challenges. Historically, you've been told there is one approach to building businesses that is influenced by short-term ROI logic. This does not solve many of your core challenges and you often end up stuck, burned out or not delivering on your aspirations. You have an opportunity to harness the advantages that are not available to larger, complex businesses with lots of owners. If you realise this, you can have a more energetic and positive view of your business beyond the short-term challenges.

Harnessing your SME advantages will lead to many benefits. As an SME Owner-Leader, if you become a succession thinker and build for the long term, you can lead the charge on making SMEs more valued and visible. And there is a trend of people searching for purposeful businesses where they can have impact. This is another opportunity you can take advantage of.

Getting started on the succession thinking journey may be difficult. I recommend establishing a new habit. In James Clear's book *Atomic Habits*, he asserts that to build new habits we need to start small. So many SME Owner-Leaders find the path out of daily demands difficult. The small habit here is to identify as a succession thinker and allocate 30 minutes a day to thinking about the principles outlined in subsequent chapters.

To become a succession thinker, you need to know what it means to be one. In the next chapter, I will introduce succession thinking and make clear what it is and what it is not. This sets up the introduction of the five principles that guide succession thinking.

## Chapter 2

# INTRODUCING SUCCESSION THINKING

## Introduction

It's 2022, and I am at breakfast with three fellow SME Owner-Leaders – Doug, Shane and Wayne. They are all succession thinkers seeking a return on vision (ROV). They want to deliver on a vision, not simply financial returns (ROI). During our meetings I can get a tad passionate about leaders who are applying ROI logic (shareholder returns) but professing they will deliver a holistic (multi-stakeholder) vision. Given this, my breakfast buddies looked nervous as I ordered a strong coffee – more rant fuel. However, this morning Doug said something that had a big impact on me: 'In 2017, I hadn't considered there was any other way than ROI. Now that I have built a company to exist, not to exit, I know ROV works.'

I reflected on my first meeting with Doug back in 2017. He was stressed. A key person had left his business, not in a way Doug was happy with. Given Doug's values, he wanted all employee exits to be of high integrity. Doug was a long-term thinker and recognised the need of capable, aligned people for the success of his business.

He was a people-first thinker. Up till this time Doug had an ROV mindset but was implementing ROI logic in his business. Doug's business, Sentient Computing, became a customer of mine and implemented succession thinking as a means of delivering ROV.

You may also be a person who has an ROV mindset but you are currently using an ROI business approach. If so, succession thinking is for you – your mindset and how you build your business will become aligned.

Let's get clear about what succession thinking is:

*Succession thinking is a method for SME Owner-Leaders to steward their business. This includes decision making as owners, directors and leaders, and how they design and build their business. Succession thinking is an approach to deliver Return on Vision.*

A key point to make here is that ROV is very well aligned with the fundamental makeup of an SME. The owners of an SME can form an authentic vision – driven by aspirations and goals – and monitor its delivery over a long period. The SME owners can support its evolution. In this capacity an SME owner can be a vision custodian. If no person or group of people is assigned accountability for vision custodianship, the probability of ROV being achieved is low. In fact, it is my observation that without the clarity of accountability for the long-term commitment to vision, a business vision defaults to ROI.

The following diagram shows why PLCs default to return on investment and find any other type of vision difficult to form and sustain.

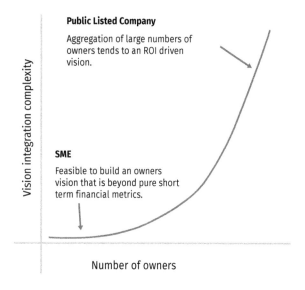

**Public Listed Company**

Aggregation of large numbers of owners tends to an ROI driven vision.

**SME**

Feasible to build an owners vision that is beyond pure short term financial metrics.

Number of owners

## ROI vs ROV

So what are the differences between ROI and ROV?

The majority of business governance is driven by short-term ROI thinking. Doug makes an excellent point: he wanted to build a business to *exist, not exit.* Doug is not saying that he would not sell his business at some stage in the future. He is saying if he has a mindset to build for the long term, he will build a better business. This business will have a higher probability of delivering dividends and higher performance.

I have facilitated many SME owner vision workshops. It is hard enough to facilitate an integrated vision across five people, let alone 1000 or 10,000.

A lot of PLC business advice and education is being applied to SMEs, centred on the ROI mindset.

An ROV mindset supports leaders to build a business that thrives beyond their tenure: as an Owner-Leader you acknowledge you are accountable for supporting the success of your successors. Within your business, stewardship encourages a more cooperative environment focused on group success. It will allow you to grow by distributing leadership to others.

## The five principles of succession thinking

Succession thinking is a way of building a business at any stage of its evolution. You can have success and create value over the long term. It is based on the implementation of five principles:

- Seek role clarity
- Build your owners' vision
- Build leadership beyond you
- Build culture beyond you
- Build your Business Way.

As a succession thinker, you will build your Business Way to maximise the probability of delivering on your vision. The application of these principles will be captured in your Business Way.

Succession thinking is not succession planning. It is a superset of succession planning. Succession thinking creates the conditions for an effective handover of all aspects of business, including roles where accountability is held, ownership and guidance. You build your business understanding that the distribution of decision rights is critical to long-term success.

*Succession thinking creates the conditions for an effective handover of all aspects of business, including roles where accountability is held, ownership and guidance.*

Succession thinking helps you build your Business Way, where you can capture and maintain the data associated with the following questions. How do you:

- form and share your guidance: owner vision, purpose and values?
- make ownership and capital decisions?
- form and implement strategy?
- organise yourself (teams and people)?
- clarify accountability to support productivity?
- systemise your business (capture how you work)?
- lead and develop tomorrow's leaders?
- embed and nurture your culture?

The answers to these questions are vital. If you have valid data for these, your business will be set up for long-term value creation.

Building the skills to become a succession thinker is a benefit to you as an SME Owner-Leader and can be applied at any stage of your evolution. Building your skills as a succession thinker will increase the probability of building a business aligned to your aspirations.

A key challenge for understanding succession thinking is to consider succession from day one. The Stephen Covey habit – *Begin with the end in mind* – informs everything you do. This does not mean the end of the business; this can be your vision as an end.

As a succession thinker your focus is on the vision, and the financial objectives are part of that vision. Financial success is also an outcome of the pursuit of delivering the vision. In short-term ROI, your vision can become dominated by shorter term financial objectives.

In this chapter, we will:

- explore the differences between succession thinking and succession planning in detail, including paths that Owner-Leaders often take that have a poor record of success
- explore what your Business Way is and how the clarity of what this is can have a big impact on your thinking as a leader of your business.

## Succession thinking is *not* succession planning

Succession *planning* targets a specific person, role or thing. As a succession *thinker*, you need to integrate succession into how you build your business.

Succession planning has been around for a long time. However, it has primarily been the remit of professionals like lawyers and accountants. Often, this is associated with their role in supporting estate planning. The focus is on a specific position or some ownership capital.

Succession planning is often oversimplified or left too late, leading to poor outcomes. It is not about simply handing over one role or some shares in the company. It is about being able to hand over the business to others in alignment with the owners' vision. As a succession thinker, you can create the conditions for succession events that have a higher probability of success.

### The GM challenge

A typical approach to succession in SMEs is the appointment of a General Manager. Often, in these cases, handover is confused with delegation. There is a lack of clarity about what decision rights and accountability have been passed on. This confusion leads to bad outcomes for the business. Owners may also have been tired and pushed below the line. While in that state, they said, 'I'm exhausted. I'm going to find a GM and they can run this place.' In doing this, they need to set the GM up for success, so clarity of the Business Way and clarity of what accountabilities are being handed over are critical.

I have supported SMEs that had problems caused by lack of clarity about their Business Way. In two cases, the founding Owner-Leaders appointed a new leader of the business, which they called a GM. In one case they included a sale of shares, so the GM was now an owner. In both cases, they did not have any clarity on their Business Way and it caused diabolical problems. The GMs were from corporations and they started installing logic from their previous companies into these SMEs. This led to near catastrophe. I helped these owners save their businesses.

Succession thinking mitigates the risk of ending up here.

You may say, 'I have seen GMs work at different organisations, so what is the problem?' The key is to determine if this is truly being executed with succession thinking or if it's simply moving key person risk from one person to another. The following questions dive a little deeper into the GM challenge:

- What accountabilities and decision rights will you hand over?
- How will you hand them over?
- How do you assess the GM's value alignment with you?
- How will your team, loyal to you, feel about a new leader?
- What happens if the General Manager gets sick or can no longer do the role?
- What ways is the General Manager introducing that override your ways?

## Activity: What needs to be handed over?

I recommend the following activity to get more consciousness about what needs to be handed over, and to raise awareness of what may happen if you do not do it wisely.

| Question | Description | Percentage |
|---|---|---|
| How important are the values of the owners to the success of the business? Record this as a percentage. A low percentage would mean that they are not important. | *What do you value?* *What makes you angry or frustrated?* *What makes you happy and satisfied?* *What behaviours are acceptable and unacceptable in your business?* | |
| You make what percentage of commercial decisions? | *Think about expenditure decisions. Who gets to spend what when?* | |
| What percentage of people are you a team leader or manager for? | *If someone wants an increase in salary, who makes the call?* | |
| What is the percentage you contribute to future strategy? | *Do you make the call on changing your product offerings or entering new markets?* | |
| What is the percentage of revenue you affect? | *Do you still sell the offering, and if so, what would happen if you did not show up tomorrow?* | |
| What percentage of commercial support do you give the company, such as debt support and guarantees? | *Do you manage the working capital of the business?* | |

| Question | Description | Percentage |
|---|---|---|
| How much knowledge do you carry regarding the offering of the business? | *Do you have knowledge about the products and services that are not shared and distributed to others?* | |
| | **Total** | A value 700 or less |
| | **Average** | Total/700 |

This is a quick review to reflect on how much there is to hand over. It underscores why there is a lot of work to set up other leaders for success. You might find it difficult to do because it can be hard to quantify these things. The key to this activity is to do the reflection.

To download this activity go to: www.successionthinking.com/activities

# What is your Business Way?

In this section I will share a holistic view of succession thinking and the development of your Business Way.[3] As your business evolves, you become more consumed by the operations of the business. You have built practices and processes that are key differentiators in your current or future success. But many of these are not explicit: they are tacit and in your or other people's heads. If the business could remain in a steady state where nothing changed, this would be fine. However, life happens to everyone and so do changes in business. Given this, what are the things you need to do so others can make sense of your SME?

---

3    This is explored in greater detail in chapter 7.

Succession thinking helps you build your Business Way, so you can capture and maintain the results of the following questions.

| How do you ... | The data to capture and maintain |
| --- | --- |
| Form and share your guidance: owner vision, purpose and values? | Owners' vision |
| | Vision statement |
| | Purpose |
| | Values |
| Make ownership and capital decisions? | Owners' vision (guidance) |
| | Owner-Director team practices and methods |
| Form and implement strategy? | Organisation team practices and methods |
| Organise yourself (teams and people)? | Organisation maps |
| | Operation team's practices |
| Clarify accountability to support productivity? | Position and role clarity |
| | Team accountability and role clarity |
| Systemise your business to capture how you work? | Maps and process guidance |
| Lead and develop tomorrow's leaders? | Organisation leader role clarity |
| | Organisation leader development |
| | Team leader role clarity |
| | Team leader development |
| Embed and nurture your culture? | Cultural leadership |
| | Values constitution |
| | Team member journey |

Your Business Way should ultimately be about delivering your owners' vision. The more you can make sense of your business, the more you can design it to deliver what you want. A primary source for strategy and culture for the business is the vision. As you will see when you explore the five principles, the vision and the context of the SME Owner-Leader need to be detailed and provide clarity to all. How do you make your Business Way as visible as possible? How do you capture your Business Way and use it to distribute leadership to others?

Succession thinking is about building your business for now *and* the future. As a succession thinker, you have a humble view of your ability to predict markets or any other future event. It is instead about being able to survive the challenges as you navigate towards your vision. The starting point for all initiatives is the vision of the Owner-Leader. Your Business Way supports the business in getting there.

The Canadian Imperial Bank of Commerce wrote a report about SME succession which stated that inadequate business succession planning was a growing macroeconomic risk:

*At this stage of the game, a small business's principal strength, the reliance on the human capital of the owner in almost every aspect of the business, is also becoming its primary weakness. Adequate succession planning requires time and is often measured in years, not days or months. Still, close to 60% of business owners age 55 to 64 have yet to start discussing their exit plans with their family or business partners.*

Part of the challenge is the reference to succession planning. A plan is like a project. It has a start and finish. Succession thinking is a way of doing things that supports the outcomes you want. Succession thinking puts you in the right place, with a more humble view of what you can control. By building and maintaining your Business Way, you will put everything in place to support succession.

A fundamental problem that must be solved for any handover to take place is building enough trust. Building trust can be difficult, and is exacerbated by:

- a lack of vision clarity
- a lack of clarity about your Business Way
- the behaviour of the Owner-Leaders (often unconscious)
- a lack of confidence in successors.

---

*A fundamental problem that must be solved for any handover to take place is building enough trust.*

---

Successful leadership succession is critical to grow a business. This problem of building trust needs to be dealt with from the start of a business. Successful handover will not take place in a low-trust environment.

### Activity: Your Business Way

Let's do a stocktake of your Business Way. This may be a hard task at this stage of the book. However, it is never too early to begin considering these issues. I provide the explanation for each data type in the activity notes.

| Your Business Way data | Where is it stored? | How is it communicated? |
|---|---|---|
| Owners' vision<br>Vision statement<br>Purpose<br>Values | | |

| Your Business Way data | Where is it stored? | How is it communicated? |
|---|---|---|
| Owner-Director team practices and methods | | |
| Organisation team practices and methods | | |
| Organisation maps<br>Operation teams practices | | |
| Position and role clarity<br>Team accountability and role clarity | | |
| Maps and process guidance | | |
| Organisation leader role clarity<br>Organisation leader development<br>Team leader role clarity<br>Team leader development | | |
| Cultural leadership<br>Values constitution<br>Team member journey | | |

To download this activity go to: www.successionthinking.com/activities

As a succession thinker, this data forms your Business Way. You may think this is a long way from your current world, where you are overwhelmed by operations. I recommend that you be patient as you read this book. The solutions will unfold. However, this highlights one of the significant challenges: it's difficult to undertake succession thinking with a technician or even an operation leadership mindset.

## Trust is essential

Prior to getting into the principles of succession thinking, it is wise to explore areas that impact your mindset and practices. If you want to build a business using short-term ROI approaches, succession thinking is not for you. However, if you want to build for the long term, building trust is essential. Trust is essential for effective handovers.

You may have an organisation chart in your business, and you may have lots of policies. If you're going to build for the long term and distribute decision rights to others, these things are up for grabs. This is about exploring your openness to change these ideas in the service of your aspirations. By leaning into understanding your mindset, you can make a clearer decision about whether succession thinking is for you.

What is your view regarding the following?

- **People in your business – do you guide or legislate?**
  If you build a business based on the assumption that 90% of people will do the wrong thing, you'll ultimately create a low-trust environment. You will probably try to legislate everything. Rules and policing do not connect well with people's desires for autonomy. To guide is to activate excellent systems to give people context.
- **The power differential you have as an SME Owner-Leader.**
  As an SME Owner-Leader, I thought of myself as a peer of people in my business – just a boy from Kununurra. However, a forthright coach told me that the power differential is there and needs

to be acknowledged. Knowing this helped me to decrease this differential.

Here's a story about power differential. In 2009 in our Perth office we hired Mary, a new geologist. I knew Mary as a customer and got on well with her. But when she was inside our business, I noted a slight change in her behaviour. One day, Mary's team leader said Mary wanted to tell me the following joke – 'How do you turn a duck into a soul singer? Put it in the microwave until its bill withers.' A harmless and funny joke. Well, to me, anyway. Mary did not think she could tell me that joke because she thought of me as the 'big boss'. For the rest of my working life as an Owner-Leader, I tried to remove this differential, while being mindful of how to lead to solve the accountability and effectiveness challenges.

- **Power hierarchy, organisation charts and reporting lines.**
Dan Pink's work on motivation shows people want autonomy, mastery and connection to a higher purpose. Your attitude towards these is important. Power hierarchies and traditional management systems erode autonomy. The design challenge to develop accountability and build trust is difficult, but this is an essential pursuit for a succession thinker.

- **Transparency.**
How do you share with your team? Trust is built by promoting transparency, because obfuscation – conscious or unconscious – undermines trust. There is still information that belongs to the individual or only certain people; a person's salary, for example. But it has been my experience that the greater the information sharing, the greater the team support in bad times. In good times, fair distribution of profits can be a challenge given the subjective nature of remuneration decisions. But it is still a better place to be.

If you pursue maximising trust and build the practices to do so, you are building a core capability of a succession thinker. Challenging the mindsets that have been in business for a hundred years is difficult, but not optional if you're handing over the leadership of your baby. By maximising trust across your company, you will allow leaders you trust to emerge. We will discuss this in more detail in chapters 5 and 6.

**Activity: Power hierarchy**

This activity reflects on power hierarchy.

Draw a picture of how your business works. Then include how you manage people. This is a resource to be used to induct new people into your business and explain how you work.

This activity highlights the challenge of maintaining accountability while maximising trust. You might find doing this difficult. SME Owner-Leaders usually have flat structures, but this activity is to get you to reflect on how the way you organise yourself has a big impact on trust.

To download this activity go to: www.successionthinking.com/activities

## Conclusion

You may look at some of these concepts and be challenged by them. They may even trigger some strong negative responses about losing control. However, that is to be expected, and implementing succession thinking therefore needs a method. The subsequent chapters discuss more about the *how*. My recommendation is that you, as the Owner-Leader, stay open and curious.

Succession thinking is a way of building your business, at any stage of its evolution, so that you can create value over the long term. Succession planning has typically been used in the latter or transition stages of a business and not as a way of building a business. In the initial stages of your business, you have a lot of accountability for selling or delivering to your customers. As a business grows, it's wise to switch the focus to the people who will deliver the value to your customers: your team. If you can clearly communicate your Business Way to the team, it empowers your business while creating the foundations for succession.

For you to lean into being a succession thinker, you need to explore practices that maximise trust. Succession is about handing over a lot of decision rights for something you care about. It's also about challenging your own ego relentlessly to allow others to flourish in their roles, including your successor.

If you are a super-curious person, lean into that. However, a risk for entrepreneurs is that they become 'knowers' – they think they know or can figure out everything. They develop this as a byproduct of the journey of perpetually finding solutions. Therefore, build new habits to challenge knower behaviour and lean into being a learner. Explore your ideas about control, trust and handover.

As an Owner-Leader, you can become overwhelmed by how many hats you have and get 'hat dizzy'. So, in the coming chapter, we explore the first principle of succession thinking: seek role clarity.

# Chapter 3

# PRINCIPLE 1:
# SEEK ROLE CLARITY

## Introduction

As a succession thinker, you need to understand where accountability and decision rights sit in your business. What roles do you have as an Owner-Leader? Investing in role clarity is a practical way to start developing your Business Way. A role is a set of accountabilities that can be executed by a person with the required skills and attributes.

You're likely to handle a broad range of tasks, from managing finances to developing and then selling the product. These tasks are distributed across several roles. As your business grows, you may not realise how many roles you are performing. They are all aggregated, which leads to problems with effectiveness and culture. Failing to clarify roles can hinder your ability to achieve your desired outcomes, as explained in chapter 1. Therefore, it's crucial to establish clear roles as your business grows.

### Positions vs roles

It's important to distinguish between a position and a role, as this difference can cause confusion. In succession thinking, a position is a specific job held by an individual with an employment or commercial agreement. A position comprises a set of roles or a role stack the individual executes. The job title reflects the position, not the roles associated with it.

This distinction is crucial because roles should define accountability, not positions. For example, in chapter 2 we discussed General Managers – GM is the title of a position, not a role. Several roles need to be performed by the person in this position. A lack of accountability clarity is why many General Managers are unsuccessful.

A common problem is the construction of job descriptions. You may have employed a person based on a job description with a set of responsibilities, but you reflect on the responsibilities 12 months later and they are different. This can lead to problems with performance and remuneration.

As an Owner-Leader, the best place to start the role clarity journey is with yourself. There are five roles that are persistent across SMEs, as shown in the following table.

| Role | Description |
| --- | --- |
| *Owner* | A person who has the decision rights for capital and vision: the vision custodian |
| *Director* | A person with legal responsibilities of the business so it can maintain a licence to operate |
| *Organisation leader* | A person responsible for the formation and implementation of strategy, healthy culture and the systemisation of the business |
| *Team leader* | A person who leads an effective team to deliver defined accountabilities |
| *Team member or Technician* | A team member who works on the team in a specific role |

It is common that you, as Owner-Leader, will have some or all of these generic roles. You'll find that your role stack is large. For instance, you may have multiple technician roles that are part of the selling and delivery of your products and services.

As a succession thinker, you acknowledge that you have different roles. The lack of visibility of these roles can create confusion for all, including you. By acknowledging this, you can apply the principle of role clarity across your business.

In chapter 1, I shared my experience of feeling completely overwhelmed in April 2003. I was working 60 hours a week. I was leading a team of people dissatisfied with the lack of clarity. This led to many problems, including:

- poor accountability
- reliance on hero efforts
- lack of clarity in our remuneration structure.

I then had a highly productive flight to the US. I shared my role clarity discoveries made on this flight with my fellow owners: Andy, Geoff and Colin. They devoted most of their time to principal technician roles, and they were under a lot of pressure and delivering hero efforts. Given this, they were not happy with the distraction when I booked the meeting offsite. Unfortunately, the only meeting room available was the ballroom at the Esplanade Hotel. We looked a tad ridiculous in this cavernous room, and this did not help my cause. This led to some initial frustration from colleagues, who kindly expressed it by saying, 'What is this corporate crap?'

However, in rapid time we got down to business. We adjusted our thinking so we could change from organising by person to organising by role. Although quite simplistic, it was transformative. We left knowing that we were all owners. Andy and I were directors, and our team leadership was better defined. We were clearer about the range of technician roles we executed. We had a long way to go, but this was a good start.

Genuine role clarity is transformative and a foundation building block for a succession thinker. In this chapter we will explore role clarity in detail. You will see how role clarity has a significant impact on leadership, decision making, daily practices and leadership development. When you apply this principle, you have started building your Business Way.

---

*Genuine role clarity is transformative and a foundation building block for a succession thinker.*

---

## Role clarity and relationships

The Owner-Leader is often 'hat dizzy' because they are performing many or all of these five generic roles that require different attributes and skills. The mindset and approach to making a strategic decision differs from sending a customer a proposal, for example. But the greatest cause of being 'hat dizzy' relates to all your business relationships that evolve via different hats. This becomes complex and confusing.

The set of relationships between different roles is more complex than the relationships between the people. As displayed in the relationship diagram below, if you have three team members, you have three relationships. When you have six team members, you have 15 relationships. This may help you understand why, when you grow from 10 to 20 people, it seems harder than you expected.

The sum of the relationships matters, especially with the impact on culture. If one team member is below the line, it can have a significant impact on the entire team.

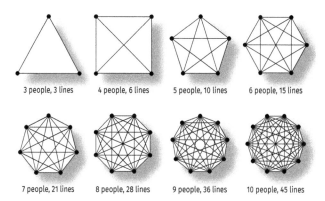

| 3 people, 3 lines | 4 people, 6 lines | 5 people, 10 lines | 6 people, 15 lines |

| 7 people, 21 lines | 8 people, 28 lines | 9 people, 36 lines | 10 people, 45 lines |

The complexity of relationships also goes up if each person has multiple roles. You, as the Owner-Leader, often have a large stack of roles.

Let's consider an example.

I interviewed the Owner-Leader of a sizable engineering business that had five owners. They did not have role clarity, but as part of the interview, I categorised the roles they had.

| Person | Roles | Role tally |
| --- | --- | --- |
| Andrew | Owner, director, organisation leader | 3 |
| George | Owner, director | 2 |
| Joan | Owner, director, organisation leader, team leader | 4 |
| Donna | Owner, technician | 2 |
| Steve | Owner, organisation leader, team leader, technician | 4 |
| | Total | 15 |

The total of roles is 15. The following equation helps make sense of the complexity:

Relationships = (Numbers of roles × (Number of roles − 1)) ÷ 2

Relationships = (15 × 14) ÷ 2 = 105

The number of relationships reduces to 88 when self-referencing is removed; that is, Steve as Owner having a relationship with Steve as Technician.

What is the potential for miscommunication between Joan and Steve? Steve could talk to Joan with her team leader hat on, but Joan perceives it to be the owner hat. After discussing this with the Owner-Leader, he could explain some tensions in recent owners' meetings.

Making sense of your roles is essential to succession thinking. Clarity is increased by having the right conversations in the right forums. Your SME may have the same challenge. You may find you are conflating roles and that is causing issues.

The following diagram shows there are three natural levels of hierarchy associated with decision making in SMEs.

### Natural Hierarchy for decision making in SMEs

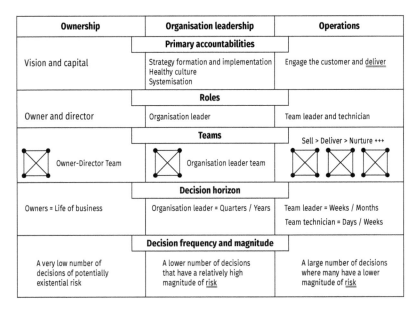

| Ownership | Organisation leadership | Operations |
|---|---|---|
| | **Primary accountabilities** | |
| Vision and capital | Strategy formation and implementation Healthy culture Systemisation | Engage the customer and deliver |
| | **Roles** | |
| Owner and director | Organisation leader | Team leader and technician |
| | **Teams** | Sell > Deliver > Nurture +++ |
| Owner-Director Team | Organisation leader team | |
| | **Decision horizon** | |
| Owners = Life of business | Organisation leader = Quarters / Years | Team leader = Weeks / Months  Team technician = Days / Weeks |
| | **Decision frequency and magnitude** | |
| A very low number of decisions of potentially existential risk | A lower number of decisions that have a relatively high magnitude of risk | A large number of decisions where many have a lower magnitude of risk |

Each team's primary purpose drives the roles that will take part. The roles have different accountabilities that will collectively deliver to the team's purpose. Although each business has its own unique characteristics, this team/role pattern is common to all.

The first team is the Owner-Director team. This team is the equivalent of the SME board. Each SME will have its own specific accountabilities for the Owner-Director team.

| Team name | Owner-Director |
|---|---|
| **Key roles** | Owner |
| | Director |
| | Adviser |
| **Purpose** | Vision and capital |
| **Typical key accountabilities** | The formation and maintenance of vision |
| | To seed the values code or constitution |
| | Manage working capital |
| | Design and develop the ownership system |
| | Form and maintain the shareholders' agreement |
| | Define the remuneration model |
| | Make profit allocation decisions |
| | Explore other entrepreneurial opportunities |
| | Execute all fiduciary responsibilities as a director |

These accountabilities contribute to answering the questions of how we fund our business and how we sustain our business. The roles of owner and director deliver these accountabilities.

The second team is the organisation leadership team. This team is the team that leads the business. It has high-level account-abilities.

| Team name | Organisation leadership |
|---|---|
| Key roles | Organisation leaders |
| | Adviser |
| Purpose | Lead the business |
| Key accountabilities | Form and implement strategy |
| | Build and maintain healthy culture |
| | Develop leadership |
| | Design how the business works |
| | Systemise the business |

The third level in this natural hierarchy are the operations teams. These are the teams that build, sell and deliver your products and services, and then nurture the products. I call these the 'customer flow' teams. These need to be understood given the unique needs of each business. The customer flow teams are supported by finance, people and culture and systemisation teams.

The specific accountabilities are unique to your business, but the accountabilities that are common to all team leaders are to lead:

- maintains trust and psychological safety
- aligns team purpose and team values
- provides effective stewardship
- provides clarity of roles
- drives meaningful progress
- requires high levels of accountability.

The succession thinking principles are building blocks. Without this role clarity building block, you will struggle to be a successful succession thinker. You may think it should be simple. As stated previously, your business is complex. Everyone in your business can also have the challenges of life. Divorce, death or illness are events that add another dimension to this complexity.

Frederic Laloux, author of *Reinventing Organizations*, differentiates complicated from complex. He asserts that organisations that are led as if they are complicated have poor outcomes. The leaders have not acknowledged that they lead a complex system. Laloux suggested that building a 747 aircraft is a complicated system. It involves a large number of individual parts and subsystems that must be assembled in a specific sequence. However, the process can be broken down into a set of clearly defined steps. These steps can be implemented by a team of experts and result in a predictable outcome.

In contrast, complex systems cannot be fully understood or controlled by any one person or group. This is because of their inherent unpredictability and emergent properties. Laloux argues that traditional organisational models, that are based on a command-and-control hierarchy, are effective for managing complicated systems. He argues they are ill-suited for dealing with complexity.

As succession thinkers, we acknowledge all organisations are complex and that complexity grows by number of people and number of roles. The advantage we can harness as SME Owner-Leaders is that we are at the simpler end of that complexity. By leaning into role clarity, we have the first building block to make sense of our businesses.

In 2018, I met John at a cafe in Fremantle. John was the Owner-Leader of a company and also the primary team leader, as well as performing several technician roles. Unfortunately, he was struggling to cope with a high turnover rate of staff and this was overwhelming him.

I explained that role clarity could be the starting point for helping John. With limited exploration and curiosity, he declared, 'It's not simple enough.' John then told me about the relationship challenges he had in his life. My reflection on this conversation was that he didn't acknowledge his business situation was complex. I wondered if there was a connection between his life challenges and understanding relationships. If you can't see the relationship complexity, poor decision making may be a result.

Your challenge of SME business is complex. Acknowledging the complexity allows you to make sense of it all. Role clarity is a practical approach to do this. You might say, 'I will do this in the future.' However, role clarity is most effective when implemented from the beginning. In doing so, you can significantly improve effectiveness. If you push the implementation into the future it becomes more difficult, and you can create inertia because the complexity has grown.

## Activity: Ownership roles

This activity will help you understand the roles held by owners in the business. Using the five generic roles, map the relationships in your business. It will give you a wonderful insight into why you may feel 'hat dizzy'.

Recognising the connections with teams is an important outcome of this activity.

To download this activity go to: www.successionthinking.com/activities

## Role clarity supports effective growth

A challenge in SMEs is how to scale effectively. If you scale people without monitoring accountability, costs can grow without a commensurate productivity increase. Having a focus on role clarity and the succession of roles will improve resourcing decisions. This supports a more resilient approach to growth. You are often faced with the challenge of assigning people to tasks they can't do well. You may do work you aren't good at. Fortunately, clarifying roles can help make sense of these issues.

Let's explore the following questions:

- How do you define a role?
- How does acumen impact role succession?
- How do you support role succession?


A role is a logical set of accountabilities that a person with a commensurate acumen can fulfil. The acumen is the union of their character attributes and their skills.

The challenge of defining roles is driven by how you distribute accountability across the business. In many parts of your business, this is more straightforward because the craft and the role align well; for instance, an accountant will be on a finance team. However, in the economic engine, there are many roles unique to your organisation.

The following is an example of a delivery coordinator role, a role to support delivering the products and services. It makes sense within the context of the business. However, the intention is to communicate the benefits that come from abstracting the role from the person.

| Role component | Details |
|---|---|
| *Key accountabilities* | Support implementers to deliver great workshops to customers |
| | Prepare the data and reports for organisation reviews |
| | Manage the DiSC profile process |
| | Administrate and troubleshoot room bookings and parking |
| | Support systems including Helpjuice, Coach Kit and Loom videos |
| | Moderate Slack |
| | Uphold compliance to guidelines |
| | Ensure timely response and support for contributors for forum participants |
| *Skills* | Document preparation (Google Docs and Word) |
| | Scheduling and prioritisation skills |
| | High-level systems literacy |
| | Experienced in a customer-focused role |
| | Understanding of our products and services |
| | Understanding of customer flow systems, including CRM |
| *Attributes* | Affable and calm |
| | Supportive and caring |
| | Attention to detail |
| | Proactive |

This is a dry way of communicating a role, but there are ways you can bring a role to life. For instance, a video recorded by the incumbent makes the communication richer. The incumbent can communicate current tasks and how they relate to these accountabilities.

A useful analogy for understanding acumen is to think of a cheetah and an eagle. Cheetahs can run at high speeds, and eagles have flight and sight. Both are exceptional in their own way. However, you may encounter cheetahs who aspire to fly or eagles who want to run at speed. To avoid these mismatches, it's crucial to be clear about the required acumen for each role. This clarity minimises the risk of hiring the wrong person for the job.

Our research on tracking people's motivation at work shows the roles they perform matter. The clarity of good fit to roles they execute is important to them. People look elsewhere if they are not happy with the work they do. A problem you may have is providing subsequent opportunities in a way sustainable to the business. By being clear about role acumen, you can have authentic conversations about someone's aspirations and their suitability for a role. Without role clarity, conversations can be difficult and the risk of losing good people increases. Role clarity will have a positive impact on the retention of good people. Given people turnover has a big impact on SMEs, role clarity is worth the effort.

Role succession provides a way to get a successor trained and productive as quickly as possible. It also helps reduce knowledge loss when a new person has been assigned to the role. You have a big risk if a key person leaves your business and they are executing without role clarity. Also, if the current person is moving to a new role, they

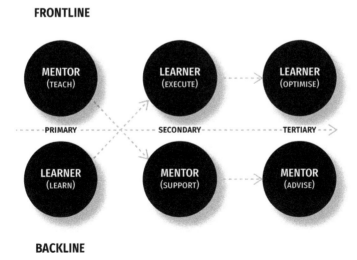

can support their successor to be more effective in a shorter period. This is all about productivity.

The above diagram communicates the process for how a role is handed over. There are two participants: the mentor and the learner. The mentor is handing over to the learner. There are three phases: primary, secondary and tertiary. During the primary phase, the mentor is still working in the role and the learner is observing. In the secondary phase, the learner is doing the role, and the mentor is supporting. In the tertiary phase, the learner is executing but can get advice from their mentor on an ad hoc basis. Having clarity about a role succession process mitigates a lot of risks in the transfer. You may not do this with all roles, but it is essential to have a process of this type for leadership roles.

Understanding the distribution of accountability across your business will underwrite sustainable growth. You can foster this by applying role clarity. This then supports high-quality conversations with people regarding their acumen and the required acumen of a role. It helps to solve the 'cheetah/eagle problem'.

---

*Understanding the distribution of accountability across your business will underwrite sustainable growth.*

---

In chapter 5 you will explore how to build leadership beyond you. It is difficult to grow sustainably without distributing leadership to others. The cheetah/eagle problem is at its greatest when we investigate leadership roles. People often have an aspiration to lead without the acumen or the desire to do the learning. By being mindful of role acumen and how to do role handover, you can increase success in distributing leadership to others.

In 2017 I attended a workshop with three individuals – Ada, Mike and Christine – who jointly owned a company. However, there was a lack of role clarity and significant misalignment, resulting in tension within the team. The confusion arose as they were unsure about the decision-making rights and responsibilities of their roles. They had poor clarity for the rights of the owners, directors and organisation leaders.

Ada took on most of the organisation leadership responsibilities. Christine did not contribute to this area. Despite this, Christine wanted to receive equal compensation. We worked hard to clarify the roles, and Christine did not have the skills for the organisation leadership role. As a result, Ada and Mike remained as owners, directors and organisation leaders, while Christine continued as owner, director and team member (technician).

Ada, Mike and Christine all wanted their business to grow, but their lack of role clarity and role acumen was a roadblock. The clarity about what was required in skills and attributes supported a good outcome for all and removed that roadblock.

You might find this overwhelming because you have to solve all of this and it's a lot of work. For you to understand the attributes and skills of all the roles in your business is huge, especially when you are busy working in operations. This is a fair and expected response. As with most recommendations in this book, the key is to start small and be patient. You are not solving a transaction of business. You are building a new practice that is part of your Business Way. If you gain more role clarity for the Owner-Leaders, you have made a tremendous start.

**Activity: Role acumen**

The following activity will help you understand this more. Reflect on your acumen for two different roles in your business. Complete the role descriptions for these two roles.

Reflect on the required skills and attributes. You may be a principal technician and think of these because of your daily demands.

Do this activity with a fellow owner or trusted adviser. This will help you discuss the accountabilities defined and also the acumen to execute these roles.

To download this activity go to: www.successionthinking.com/activities

## Conclusion

In this chapter, you have learned that the generic roles in an SME are owner, director, organisation leader, team leader and technician. You, as an Owner-Leader, will have several – and often all – of them. Getting clear about roles is the starting point to becoming a succession thinker.

Your business is complex because it is made up of the relationships between people in the business who then connect to customers and other stakeholders. Each of these people then has several roles. If something happens to a person who is critical to the business, without role clarity, this is very challenging.

Your extensive set of roles can make it particularly difficult for you and your team. Clarity can increase effectiveness and support getting time back. Even though your business is complex, it is small, so you can overcome the complexity and make it simpler. As a succession thinker, you can grow sustainably by becoming clearer about how accountability is distributed across your business. You can solve this by applying role clarity. This then supports high-quality conversations with people regarding their acumen and the required acumen of a role. It helps to solve the cheetah–eagle problem.

The cheetah–eagle problem is at its greatest when we investigate leadership roles. People often have an aspiration to lead without the acumen or the desire to do the learning. By being mindful of role acumen and how to do role handover, we can increase success in distributing leadership to others.

In the next chapter, you will be able to immerse yourself in the role of the owner. You will explore a key accountability of being an owner: building the owner vision.

# Chapter 4
# PRINCIPLE 2:
# BUILD YOUR OWNERS' VISION

## Introduction

In this chapter, we will explore one of the core accountabilities of being an owner: crafting and maintaining your vision. The vision makes sure the business delivers your goals and aspirations while also delivering the promise to your customers and the team. One of the SME advantages is you have only a few owners, so it is possible to craft the vision among you. This becomes difficult as the number of owners increases. The vision can be truly authentic and can be inclusive for all stakeholders of your business.

The owners' vision is the manifesto of the business. It includes guidance for the succession of ownership and what you want for all stakeholders in the future. Having a well-understood and integrated owners' vision will help you to make good capital decisions about future ownership, capital for growth and the variable rewards of remuneration. An owners' vision supports the decision-making framework for these. To connect to the customers, you will derive a vision statement that communicates more about your products and services.

You can build your business on return on vision instead of short-term ROI logic. This underwrites the long-term nature of succession thinking. Economist Mariana Mazzucato wrote a book called *The Value of Everything*. She references the terms 'value creation' and 'value extraction'. Building a business with an ROV mindset will drive strategies for value creation, not value extraction. The owners' vision is the first building block of your Business Way. The decision rights of each owner are directly related to the percentage of shares they own. People who have these rights are called vision custodians.

When I went 10-pin bowling with my kids, I put the rails up so the ball didn't end up in the gutter. It was embarrassing having my bowls going in the gutter as my kids kept striking. A well-implemented owners' vision provides the guardrails for your business. An example of a gutter ball in business is where the business does something in contravention of your fundamental values. The guardrails can be there as you hand over decision rights and are less hands on.

In July 2022, I was in a workshop room interviewing Brett, the founder and Owner-Leader of Mine Survey Plus. Brett was a prospective customer of ADAPT by Design. This was only the second time we had met, so I did not know Brett well. I asked him to tell me what his primary motivations were for building Mine Survey Plus and how he derived satisfaction. He said, 'I get my satisfaction from seeing the people in my business get to their professional and financial objectives.' I immediately knew I was talking to a person with a clear vision for his business – we just had to assist with making it explicit. Mine Survey Plus became a customer, and when they built their values constitution, one of their values was: *put family first*. This is shown below.

### Put family first

*Our meaning: You only get one crack at being a parent, one opportunity to bury your 15-year-old Border Collie under the lemon tree who gave you the shits but was a 'very good boy – yes he was – what a good boy'.*

*Life happens, and that's ok! Be there for your family and friends when they need you, especially your life partner, kids, parents and siblings. Don't miss out on the big moments or the special days, say yes to the travel opportunities ... this stuff is important! It is more important than work and that is why you have options around which leave to take (annual leave, leave without pay, personal leave, parental leave, I quit and am taking a job in Antarctica leave!).*

*Take the best version of yourself home after each swing. Look after yourself, use the Employee Assistance Program (EAP), and don't be afraid to lean on your peers when the going gets tough.*

*Nobody has ever laid on their deathbed wishing they spent more time at work!*

The foundation for this value is the owners' vision. This is just one component of a larger vision but it is core to Brett's motivation.

Your owners' vision sets the guidance and guardrails for your business. Brett had a good implicit vision. However, if not made explicit, it can't be used to establish guardrails.

In this chapter, we will explore the vision–capital interface and where entrepreneurship sits in your business. This helps to explain the importance of an owners' vision. So far, we have mostly considered if there is one owner. But what are the risks to your business if you have multiple owners with different visions? How do you build an integrated vision?

## Your owners' vision and decision making

The *Oxford English Dictionary* definition of an entrepreneur is:

*A person who sets up a business or businesses, taking on financial risks in the hope of profit.*

Let's use this base and expand it as a succession thinker. A person who sets out to build a product or service and will deploy capital commensurate with the risk they want to take. The person's commitment to the problem is directly connected to the risk. Therefore, the owners' vision describes the level of commitment and also gives information about what sort of capital they will deploy.

You manage your capital using debt instruments or by providing equity in the business. There are many ways of doing this, but both are potential existential threat decisions. So what is the guidance system for those decisions? The owners' vision becomes your entrepreneurial decision support system. In chapter 2, I've referenced owners who made unwise decisions about handover of ownership. They had no decision support system. The greater your ownership of a business, the greater rights you have to the vision – there is a direct relationship between equity capital and the vision for your business. Finding aligned investors is therefore very important. There is enormous risk in business, and without clarity of your vision, it will be difficult to recruit aligned investors.

Your decisions about capital will have a big impact on your capacity to think long term, and your working capital is directly affected by:

- funds raised through equity
- funds raised through debt

- the level of your remuneration spend (often greater than 80% of total expenditure)
- your approach to profit distribution or profit allocation.

It is at the vision–capital interface where you decide to become a succession thinker. Do you have an ROI mindset (short-term ROI) or an ROV mindset (long-term sustainable ROV)?

### Vision-Capital Interface

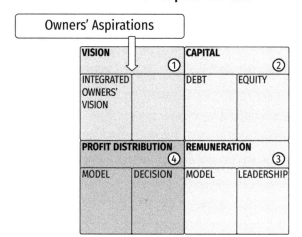

Your owners' vision provides the guardrails for capital and cultural decision making – decisions that have a big impact on the existential viability of the business and how the business interacts in the world. It covers everything from who will be a future owner to how you appoint leaders to how the team is remunerated. In succession thinking, the vision is the decision support system for the big decisions.

In the period between 1996 and 2014, acQuire – the geoscience software company I led that operated in the resources industry – traversed a marketplace where there were three significant bust events interspersed by boom events. We operated in a marketplace where the salaries would get to unsustainable levels and we could not and would not compete on money alone. We did not want to set salaries and then have to retrench people. It drove many creative ideas for how to compete in a boom. Our consciousness of the long-term impact on the capital of remuneration decisions was critical to our success. We did not call it a vision at the time, but the long-term approach to capital decision making was an example of us using an owners' vision to make the big decisions.

*Your owners' vision provides the guardrails for capital and cultural decision making – decisions that have a big impact on the existential viability of the business and how the business interacts in the world.*

Creating an explicit vision that supports long-term decision making is essential. In the acQuire example, if we had followed the market, we would have had major cultural problems in the next bust. Given the high remuneration costs, we would have had to execute cutbacks that were against our values. Our implicit owners' vision worked and provided guardrails.

The next step was to make it explicit.

You might think that constructing a vision with enough detail to guide big financial decisions is difficult. Couple this with the inherent cynicism that prevails around visioning and this idea might challenge you. However, I'll provide more logic and a practical approach in the rest of this chapter.

### Activity: The vision–capital interface

The following reflection exercise will help you explore how vision and capital are related.

| Questions | Answers |
|---|---|
| How do you find the intersection between your life aspirations and your business? | |
| How do you make capital decisions in your business? | |
| How do you make remuneration decisions? | |
| How do you make profit allocation decisions? | |
| How do you currently document your owners' vision? | |

You might find this activity difficult to do without a mentor or adviser as a sounding board. It is often difficult to do without help from someone who understands the vision–capital interface.

To download this activity go to: www.successionthinking.com/activities

# Multiple owners and an integrated vision

When you are not the only owner and you and your co-owners are not aligned, expect to see a significant fall in the value of your company. Crafting and ratifying an integrated owners' vision helps to mitigate this risk. If there is one owner and one vision custodian, you are alone, but at least there is only one decision maker. The challenge of doing this with multiple owners is exponentially more difficult.

If you are one of several owners, what could you discover when forming an integrated owner vision? The discovery might be that it is not possible because you and your colleagues want the business to deliver entirely different things. One owner may want to have a liquidity event in four years and another person may want the business for the long term.

To understand how we go about developing an integrated owners' vision, let's explore the crafting of one. The key is to agree on a set of core stakeholder groups that are important to all owners. These include:

- you
- customers
- employees
- leaders in the business
- partners
- fellow owners
- future owners
- suppliers
- community
- environment.

This is just to name a few. In many companies, there can be greater than 10 stakeholder groups.

The next step is to explore what you want for each group. Write a letter from the future where you have achieved what you want for each group. Write in the past tense as if you have arrived at the destination.

In the following table I have provided an idealistic and simple example as a succession thinker.[4]

| Stakeholder group | Vision |
| --- | --- |
| *Me* | It is great to kick back and have a lot more time to explore other opportunities. Having no operational or organisation leadership roles has given me a lot of time back. I love my connection to the business as an Owner-Mentor. Our financial success has nailed my debts and I don't have any financial anxiety. |
| *Owners* | I was so happy to see my fellow owners get their financial day in the sun, funded by the business's ability to produce sustained dividend returns while we still invested in the future. The establishment of an ownership model allowed others to invest in the custodian's vision and derive the benefits. |
| *Our customers* | *This is where you document what you want for your product and service offering. Given the bespoke nature of this, it has not been documented.*<br><br>Our measures of customer satisfaction are very high, and it is so rewarding to see our foundation customers are still with us. |
| *Our leaders* | The organisation leaders have been percolated through our business and have an extraordinary grasp of our Business Way. The vision has strengthened and continues to provide the guardrails for our business. |
| *Our people* | We could build a culture based on intrinsic motivation and maximise trust while avoiding groupthink. Healthy conflict prevails. Our value seeds underwrite our culture and are the reason we are a no-bullshit company.<br><br>Our value seeds are:<br><br>[Value seed 1]<br><br>[Value seed 2]<br><br>[etc.] |
| *Society* | *Given the bespoke nature of this, it has not been documented.* |
| *Environment* | *Given the bespoke nature of this, it has not been documented.* |

---

4    More examples – including ADAPT by Design examples – can be found at: www.successionthinking/activities/vision.

An owner vision is personal and, if done correctly, is the authentic reflection of what the owner wants. Like all new practices, it takes time to craft a vision to be authentic and implementable.

Each owner develops their vision so it truly reflects their aspirations. Each owner may have a totally different vision, but it is wise to give each other grace and honour each other's vision. This will show where the alignments and non-alignments sit.

This can be difficult to do without facilitation because you are in a business marriage and you probably did not do this at the establishment of the marriage. However, this is a fulfilling exercise, and each owner has something special to contribute to enrich the integrated owners' vision. Nothing threatens the success of a business more than non-alignment of the owners. Every decision will be affected if you do not get this clear. If you do everything to build aligned guidance with an integrated vision, you are taking a solid step towards supporting your business to flourish.

In 2021, I was working with three owners, Jeff, Mary and Ron. To begin the vision work, the founder, Jeff, had sold 8% to each of the other two with a vendor finance model. They were all organisation leaders. This process, coupled with some other discoveries, uncovered that they had different aspirations. Jeff has now bought back the 16%. If Jeff had an owner vision to support the original share sale process, it's unlikely the shares would've been sold.

You might say these are just words and it's difficult to implement or bring an owner vision to life – and it certainly can be. So I recommend that the role of vision custodian is added to your shareholders' agreement. The integrated owners' vision then becomes a schedule of the agreement. This is bespoke and will be unique to each SME. However, this will maximise clarity and mitigate risk when recruiting new owners. (The next three principles, covered in chapters 5 through 7, examine how your owners' vision can be embedded in your business.)

### Activity: Build your owner vision

This activity will help you build your owner vision.
1. Define the stakeholder groups of your business.
2. Think of a person who is a good representative of each group.
3. Write a letter from the future in the past tense to each group stating what you want as an outcome.

To download this activity go to: www.successionthinking.com/activities

This activity is difficult. It connects back to the validity of the cynicism about visioning. The idea of sitting in the future and doing some creative writing to build a story in the past tense sounds weird. To get in the right mindset, you must 'park the car'. Find a place where you'll not be distracted for hours, get relaxed and give yourself time to think.

It is worth it.

## Potential barriers to realising your vision

There are many challenges and obstacles that can get in the way. This book is about helping you maximise the probability of achieving your vision by building a business that can do it.

One common barrier is the owner's unconscious behaviours.

In 2009, I wanted to hand over all my operation leadership to focus on organisation leadership – as Michael Gerber, author of

*The E-Myth*, asserted, working *on* the business, not *in* it. Many of the concepts in this book were founded by doing this. I sensed we had some problems with our leadership and we needed to lean into this. I had just read a book by Fred Kofman called *Conscious Business*. Many of the concepts resonated with me so I sent Fred an email to share my thoughts. Fred introduced me to Mark Burrell, who was a leadership coach at Axialent, the company Fred co-founded.

In 2010, Mark – with another leadership coach, Tess Thulstrup – worked with the acQuire Leadership team. On a retreat in York, Western Australia, we made a big breakthrough. We were doing some role play, and I was a participant. Mark observed something in my behaviour and stopped the room. He asked me if I would take part in a 'fishbowl' exercise. Each of the 12 leaders in the room would give me feedback about my behavioural challenges. I agreed. This became another one of those days where you drag your schoolbag home. It was hard to cop so much feedback in that form, but it was very important. I discovered I was an unconscious knower, taking too much of the oxygen in the room. I would cut off people's learning opportunities because I was not curious enough about certain opinions. Sometimes I would not let people finish a sentence. The 360° data I received from the leadership circle work also validated this finding.

I did not like this behaviour, and I wanted to change. My initial solution was to state clearly that I needed a 'passion intervention system'. On returning to the room the following day, I shared the passion intervention system idea. We all agreed that if I was acting as an unconscious knower, they could call PIS. (This was a little unfortunate as a code.) On hearing PIS, my mantra was to detach, pause and ask a question.

I will suffer from the PIS challenge till the day I die. My friends still talk about putting raincoats on to deal with the spray when my passion is up. However, it helped me align my behaviour to my aspirations. No one was going to stick around and be my successor if I did not do something about this. To be frank, it embarrassed me and I knew it was worth the effort to change.

In Viktor Frankl's book *Man's Search for Meaning*, he says:

*When we are no longer able to change the situation – we are challenged to change ourselves.*

In short, your behaviour will have a big impact on your success at bringing your vision to life. You will fall off the horse, but making the effort around your own behaviour is worth it.

## Conclusion

Your owner vision is the foundation of building your Business Way. It provides guidance for your business and shapes your decision-making process. It serves as a manifesto for your business. You will be in a better position to decide about future ownership, growth and compensation. Rather than focusing solely on short-term ROI, you can build your business around the concept of ROV. As a succession thinker, you can create a sustainable business that creates value over the long term.

By crafting a clear owner vision, you'll be better equipped to develop effective long-term strategies. For businesses with multiple owners, an integrated owners' vision can help align interests. For single owners, having a clearly defined owner vision is crucial to mitigating risks associated with expanding ownership and non-alignment.

Investing time and effort in defining your vision is crucial to ensuring your business delivers what you want. Whether your goal is to achieve more discretionary time, growing the business or pursuing other objectives, decision making starts with your vision.

The message about behaviour is very important to succession thinking. To be successful as a succession thinker you must invest in supporting the development of people's capabilities – helping them achieve their aspirations while you achieve yours. Investing in the consciousness of how your behaviours affect others is worth it in all areas of life, not just business.

---

*To be successful as a succession thinker you must invest in supporting the development of people's capabilities – helping them achieve their aspirations while you achieve yours.*

---

Finally, stop thinking people can read your mind about your vision. Start by getting your vision documented. Then investigate how it can be used in updating or supporting the construction of your shareholders' agreement. It can be the specification you hand the lawyers.

In the next chapter, we will explore leadership in the SME context, and how you can create the conditions to distribute leadership to others.

# Chapter 5

# PRINCIPLE 3: BUILD LEADERSHIP BEYOND YOU

## Introduction

Many SME Owner-Leaders are reluctant leaders. Given they don't identify as leaders, many don't have good leadership practices in their business. To be a succession thinker, building leadership is critical.

As a succession thinking Owner-Leader, you also want others to lead. They will then have decision rights and accountabilities that you have handed over to them. To execute on this, you need a willing successor and you need to be a willing mentor. High levels of trust underwrite this. You may have started this business as a technician, so often only you have developed the knowledge of the total system. You know the nooks and crannies of your business. Other leaders coming in will rarely have the same insights into the whole system because they have entered a specific part of your business.

Developing effective organisation leaders is critical to success as a succession thinker. Building a team of organisation leaders allows you to challenge the single successor concept. You will have a solution to the successor of the successor if this is done well. Developing a team of leaders who are accountable for the whole system is antifragile. Nassim Nicholas Taleb wrote a book by this name, and although the book posits a lot more, I think the term is appropriate here. If only one individual is accountable for your business and they are incapacitated, you are in a bad place.

Building the skills to become a good organisation leader is a life pursuit. Establishing highly effective SME organisation leaders of your Business Way is the road to excellence.

Appointing an external leader to your organisation's leadership team without care can be a big risk. Percolate your leaders, don't helicopter them in. Develop leaders who are the full bottle on your Business Way, and who are homegrown as opposed to helicopter leaders who are placed on top. Understanding and developing good team leadership is a pursuit of organisation leaders. Each team member's productivity is directly related to the effectiveness of the team. Therefore, team leaders are critical to building your Business Way. Recruiting new people who have good leadership acumen can be done at the team level. However, their induction needs to be done understanding that they do not know your Business Way.

Success for you as a succession thinker is when you hand over roles you no longer want to do. This will not happen without understanding how leadership works in your business. The critical path to delivering on your vision is distributing leadership to others. By being conscious of the problems with single leaders or leaders who don't know your Business Way, you can distribute leadership with less risk.

It's a winter day in South Perth in 2017. I am sitting with Jake in a cafe – yes, another cafe. It seems to be the common meeting place.

Jake is the owner of a strata management company, he is 70 years old and he is in a bind. He is the owner of the business but three years previously he appointed a General Manager. The GM was not an owner of the business but had been given an enormous amount of authority. There was no clarity of roles, and over the three years the GM had started accumulating decision rights and was building his own Business Way. Although the business was stable financially, the culture at the time was toxic. Also, it was not resilient because Jake was fearful that the business would fall over if the GM left. The GM was building an autocracy where there was centralisation of decision rights and no development of leadership.

We helped Jake recover the business on behalf of the family and then helped Jake build the Business Way. The GM left in early 2018 as we developed greater clarity of values and vision. The business now has clarity between organisation leadership and team leadership. The leadership team replaced the GM. In October 2023 we will have a celebratory dinner to celebrate that a good part of Jake's vison has been met. The guests include the organisation leaders that helped build the Business Way and the supporting coach.

The key message of this story is what happens when you appoint a single person who is not aligned. You can mitigate a lot of risk and pain by taking a succession thinking approach.

In this chapter, we will explore:
- distributing leadership
- antifragile leadership
- percolating your leaders.

We will also dive into the acumen and challenges of organisation leadership and team leadership.

## Distributing leadership

In the previous chapter, the subjects of your vision and behaviour were discussed. Sustained financial success, growth and more discretionary time for the owner(s) cannot be achieved sustainably without handing over decision rights. As the report by the Canadian Imperial Bank of Commerce (referenced in chapter 3) stated, 'a small business's principal strength – the reliance on the human capital of the owner in almost every aspect of the business – is also becoming its primary weakness. Adequate succession planning requires time and is often measured in years, not days or months. Still, close to 60% of business owners aged 55 to 64 have yet to start discussing their exit plans with their family or business partners.'

Where do you start? Handing over technician roles first, especially those roles you're struggling with, makes sense. Finance is often a good place to start. However, this raises a tension that is common in SMEs. The Owner-Leader is often a principal technician of the business's products and services. If coupled with having no desire to be a team leader, this can create a lot of inertia for handover. Given all of this, the place to start is to build an organisation's leadership team. This team can then deal with the problem of designing solutions and decide how to extricate the Owner-Leader.

It is wise to begin with a small nucleus – potentially the Owner-Leaders only. If you have not consciously acted as an organisation leader, you can do the learning first. This will give you the knowledge of who is a good fit. This mitigates the risk of the cheetah-eagle problem. Part of your learning will be to raise the awareness that you have a Business Way.

## Systems thinking

You may have started this business as a technician and developed the knowledge of your total system. You have done everything from bank reconciliations to product development. The empirical training you received about the business as a total system is valuable. Unfortunately, others will not get that opportunity. You need to understand organisation leadership at some level to hand it over to others. If you nominate someone to be an organisation leader with no training, this is an enormous risk and can destabilise your business. This is one of the unusual conundrums of SMEs. The on-the-job training you have had in the interdependencies of your business gives you an understanding of your system. What you have been learning is systems thinking. You understand the challenges of different parts of your business and how they interoperate.

### LINEAR VS. SYSTEMS THINKING

| Linear Thinkers | Systems Thinkers |
| --- | --- |
| Break things into component pieces | Are concerned with the whole |
| Are concerned with content | Are concerned with process |
| Try to fix symptoms | Are concerned with the underlying dynamics |
| Are concerned with assigning blame | Try to identify patterns |
| Try to control chaos to create order | Try to find patterns amid the chaos |
| Care only about the content of communication | Care about content but are more attentive to interactions and patterns of communication |
| Believe organisations are predictable and orderly | Believe organisations are unpredictable in a chaotic environment |

It is important to underscore that succession thinking is a way of building a long-term business. If you are conscious of systems thinking from the beginning, you can be mindful of interdependence as you build your business. The table linear vs systems thinking attempts to display what systems thinking is. You may do a lot of this, and it is not intended to be intimidating. However, it might explain why you have intuitions about your business that are at odds with traditional management.

Systems thinking is an extensive area of learning. Engaging with it at a high level will help with developing organisation leaders. Later in this chapter, we will explore the critical customer flow of your business, from how you engage your customer to the delivery of your products and services. A more linear understanding of business is to build a set of departments as component pieces and then build an organisation chart for reporting. In this linear world, a manager is given KPIs to optimise their department, independent of the total system.

The bar is higher for how to organise your business because of the long-term nature of your business. You need to design your business to create sustained value. Most people hired into your business will enter with skills and a particular craft – marketing, finance or product building, for instance. They then need to understand their roles and how to execute their craft in your business. However, it is difficult to get them trained in understanding the nuances of other parts of the business. This is a problem that needs to be acknowledged.

How you organise your business has a big effect on the culture of the business. Good organisation leaders have knowledge, cross-organisation empathy and the accountability to deliver the vision.

If you are a succession thinker, you have built for the long term. An essential accountability is to maximise trust. Organisation charts and departments enforce power hierarchies, which undermine trust.

## Beginning the distribution of leadership

The way to begin the distribution of leadership is to start with the role of organisation leader. By making sense of this role for yourself, you can then consider the training of others. An accountability of an organisation leader is to create and implement strategies in service of the vision. They have an obligation to the long-term success of the business.

The article 'Exploring Distributed Leadership in the Small Business Context' by Jason Cope, Steve Kempster and Ken Parry (published in the *International Journal of Management Reviews*) explored distributed leadership in the small business context, finding:

> We have identified in this article that entrepreneurial teams are more likely than lone entrepreneurs to generate greater growth. The reasons appear to relate to a distribution of resources and social capital, plurality of experience, and enhanced capability for sense-making and problem-solving. We can conclude that distributed leadership is closely associated with these contributions to growth and have argued in this article that distributed leadership might assist with the growth of established SMEs.

This article explores the challenge of distributing leadership in SMEs. The authors conclude SMEs have a higher probability of greater growth through distributing leadership. As a succession thinker, you can begin the distribution of leadership by building the role of organisation leader. You are the first person to have the role and to understand its place in your Business Way. A structured handover can then be executed and you are on the road to distributed leadership. You may not even be a very good organisation leader. Your own acumen may not line up well. However, this is the starting point.

You may have some anxiety about doing the learning to become an organisation leader. Given your daily demands, this makes sense. However, we have an expression: 'You need to lean in to lean out.' You need to do this role because it's the starting point. You will find others can develop in these roles, and many will do them better than you. However, it all starts with the Owner-Leader. You have three distinct roles as an Owner-Leader. These are: owner, director and organisation leader.

## Antifragile leadership

Mitigate the risk of fragile leadership by building a team of organisation leaders who can cover all functions of your business. Each organisation leader is accountable for a part of the business but thinks as a total system leader. The organisation leadership team delivers the vision and is accountable for:

- Leading and embedding culture.
  - How do we behave?
- Forming and implementing strategy.
  - Where are we going?
  - What do we do – and what *don't* we do?
  - How will we succeed?

- Systemisation of how we work.
  - Who needs to do what – how we organise ourselves?
- Developing leaders, and leaders of tomorrow.
  - How will we sustain our business?

---

*Mitigate the risk of fragile leadership by building a team of organisation leaders who can cover all functions of your business.*

---

Historically, there has been a concept of the leader of the business – a CEO or a General Manager – having accountability for the whole business. However, if you want to build for the long term, you need a team approach where each member of the team has the mindset of the CEO. Thinking about a team of organisation leaders allows for people to cover all functions of the business while simultaneously building their systems thinking skills about the whole system. There will still be a team leader, as with all teams in your system.

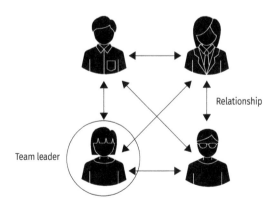

**Team diagram**

A simple but powerful concept is to draw teams in a plan, not cross section, as shown above. In this team there are four people and six relationships. It assists people in thinking about peer-to-peer relationships and reduces hierarchical thinking. By doing this, all leaders are developing cross-business understanding. If any team member is unavailable or incapacitated, the others can continue to run the show. This makes the business more resilient and avoids key person risk. To be clear, these are not operational leaders.

The ideal attributes of an organisation leader are:

- **a player:** a person who owns their behaviour and delivers their tasks
- **a learner:** a person curious regardless of how much they know.[5]

Everyone falls off the horse, but these are the ideal attributes. There is a wide range of skills to be an organisation leader. The list below is intimidating, and few people have the skills to deliver all of them.

- Build proficiency to lead the vision and purpose.
- Mentor people in the business about values and how they can support decision making.
- Build trust and accountability.
- Lead by sense-making communication in a specific form.
- Form strategy.
- Implement strategy.
- Design the business to be effective.
- Lead the systemisation of business to build role clarity and capture knowledge.

---

5    These terms are paraphrased from the book *Conscious Business* by Fred Kofman.

- Optimise the whole, recognising interdependence.
- Develop the leaders of tomorrow.

Few leaders develop skills in all these areas. It is aspirational. It may take 5 to 10 years to build some of these. However, the business will get the benefit in the near term of the development of these skills. Building the skills to become a good organisation leader is a life pursuit. If you can develop organisation leaders with these skills and attributes to build your Business Way, excellence is assured.

There are extensive risks in appointing an external leader to your team. You are now seeing how much is in your Business Way: vision, purpose, values, the strategy formation method, the strategy implementation method, approach to systemisation, design of your business to engage the market. The list goes on.

Now let's appoint a leader from the outside and give them decision rights. Have they got the skills to do this? Do they understand this information before acting? Reflect on the General Manager examples in chapter 2. If this is all implicit, how can the General Manager get started? The best place to learn about your Business Way is in situ. The organisation leadership team learns together, which contributes to a collaborative leadership approach. This develops out of the pragmatic reality that SMEs have daily demands. The organisation leaders in training are vital to supporting those in other roles.

Building an organisation leadership team, where each member can develop their organisation leadership skills, is the path to delivering your vision. The people on this team are your peers who can maximise the probability of success. The development of a collaborative organisation leadership team is antifragile and will serve you better than a nominated single leader. All training is in situ because of the daily demands of your business.

One skill I talked about was building awareness of the business as a system. This directly relates to the domain of systems thinking. I recommend a video on YouTube called 'Systems Thinking' with Dr Russell Ackoff, a leader in this area. He uses great metaphors to explain that your business is a system made up of interdependent parts. He then shares five principles of systems. Although all five are wonderful guidance for organisation leadership, I have shared the three that I think are critical.

According to Ackoff, the first principle is that the essential property of the system cannot be delivered by any of its constituent parts. A car is a system made up of parts like an engine or the wheels. Neither of these parts can transport you. Only as a unity of all the parts can it deliver the property of transporting you. His second principle is that when a system is disassembled, it loses its essential properties. A system is the product of its interactions. The third principle we will consider is that you cannot optimise separate parts without consideration of their interdependencies.

The following examples display the value of systems thinking to an organisation leader.

- You can't optimise the sales team in isolation from the delivery team. They're interdependent. A common idea is that commission selling is a good idea when selling knowledge products and services. This local optimisation will create a system flaw.
- If you put culturally aligned people into poorly designed processes that they have no control over, the outcome will be poor. The organisation of your business is a systems thinking problem because culture and accountability are interdependent.

- The place where a problem presents itself is not necessarily where you will find the solution. You may have a crisis in the delivery team. They may have been overwhelmed, but all the problems are being caused by overselling or poor expectation management by the sales team.

- Systems thinking drives us to give people context for the work they do. Knowing how a team member affects the entire system means they can provide feedback for its improvement.

Given you have a system at the small end of the scale, you can do this. You might think, 'I run an under-resourced SME. This feels too aspirational for me. Is this even possible, given my daily demands?' The following diagram is a simple way of thinking about transitions. It helps challenge impatience and supports a mindset that building new practices, habits and ways requires patience. A conscious transition approach helps with expectations for all and maximises the potential for success.

The key here is to be patient and get started. Impatience will be your enemy. To build the practices and skills of organisation leadership will take time, but you will get wins faster than you think. Getting started is the challenge.

## Conscious transition

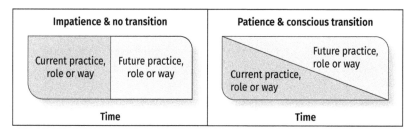

## Activity: You as an organisation leader

The following activity provides reflection about you as an organisation leader.

Using the scale below, rate yourself against each of the following leadership questions.

| 1 | Never | 2 | Rarely | 3 | Sometimes | 4 | Most of the time | 5 | Always |
|---|-------|---|--------|---|-----------|---|------------------|---|--------|

| Questions | Rating |
|-----------|--------|
| I have set a clear strategy with goals and objectives that are well communicated to everyone. | |
| I set targets for myself and the team that stretch us but are not unachievable. | |
| I look for opportunities to improve and innovate what we do and how we do it. | |
| I understand our organisation is a system and do my best to make decisions with that mindset. | |
| I actively seek ideas from my peers, our employees and customers on how we can innovate and do things better. | |
| I am prepared to hold others accountable for unproductive behaviours and actions. | |
| I clearly communicate the company direction and priorities regularly. | |

Reflect on your scores and ponder what you can do to improve in the areas that need it.

To download this activity go to: www.successionthinking.com/activities

## Percolating your leaders

Build the capacity to percolate your leaders who are the full bottle on your Business Way. Develop leaders inside the business who have filtered through your business.

In the roles outlined in chapter 3, there are two types of leaders: organisation leaders who have the remit for the total business, and team leaders who lead a team. Team leaders are critical to building your Business Way because productivity is directly related to team effectiveness. Each team needs to deliver on their account-abilities. To do this, you need to build effective teams. This requires developing team leaders. The attributes and skills of team leaders vary as a function of the purpose of each team. However, there is a common set of attributes that supports the effectiveness of the team:

- maintains trust and psychological safety
- aligns team purpose and team values
- provides effective stewardship
- provides clarity of roles
- drives meaningful progress
- requires high levels of accountability.

Being clear about the generic requirements of the team leader role empowers the development of team leaders. Developing team leaders with these skills is an essential part of building your Business Way. The people accountable for the development of team leaders are the organisation leaders. As stated in the introduction, the best way to learn is by doing. The organisation leadership team supports this learning.

There is a risk described in the article 'Exploring Distributed Leadership in the Small Business Context' (mentioned earlier in this chapter) around the relationship between the team and the Owner-Leaders. The helicopter approach does not acknowledge the close relationship of people to the Owner-Leader(s). Therefore, developing new team leaders needs to be done mindfully.

It can be chaotic and disruptive to have a team leader installing their previous company's ways. This does not mean that new ideas are not welcome. Innovation of your Business Way is essential, but unconscious mergers of many ways create chaos and non-alignment. The percolate idea is that all organisation leadership succession comes from existing team leaders. A percolation approach can also set up the successor of the successor.

All people are connected to your business via a team leader. It is common that many team members are connected to you. As an organisation leader, you can lean into developing your team leader role and your capability to execute it. You can then hand it over to others. By building team leaders, you can percolate leadership and build tomorrow's organisation leaders.

In 2010, I was an Owner-Leader of acQuire and we were looking for a regional leader of finance – a team leader. We stated we were looking for a certified practising accountant or a chartered accountant. The role was based in Perth. We had a great relationship with Claudia, the account manager who was working for the bank we used. Claudia had been in that role for six years. Dave (our global leader of finance and an organisation leader) and I had a high opinion of Claudia and we were keen for her to join us if an opportunity arose.

Claudia was an economist by training and so she had eliminated herself as a candidate for the regional accounting role. She sat in on a presentation I gave on the business. I spoke as much about leadership and culture as I did about products and commercial successes. Claudia was attracted to our business, not because of what we did, but what we stood for and how we wanted to build our business. She joined us and worked as the regional leader of finance.

Claudia soon discovered that our cultural and leadership intent was authentic, but we still had cultural challenges. However, she was connected to our way and wanted to learn about it and then support its innovation. Dave handed his organisation leader role over to Claudia in 2013 using the transition mentor approach. Dave could work in another role that was growing because of our decision to build ADAPT By Design.

The summary of this story is that Claudia entered as a team leader and learnt the acQuire Way. She was percolated to the organisation leadership role having gained a knowledge of the acQuire Way.

You may have the challenge that your business comprises technicians good at their jobs but few people possess the skills to lead teams. This is a common problem. How do you get leadership acumen into your business? Pragmatism is key. You want to percolate leaders. Organisation leaders are appointed from within wherever possible, but hiring team leaders who can then be inducted into your Business Way is a good approach.

---

*You may have the challenge that your business comprises technicians good at their jobs but few people possess the skills to lead teams. This is a common problem.*

---

Your SME may be at an early phase of evolution and you have skilled technicians but few people with aspirations for leadership or natural leadership acumen. Here, you'll need to build an organisation leadership team and recruit from the outside onto this team. The key is to have enough of your Business Way documented so you can guide your organisation leader team members. Building your owners' vision and values is enough.

## Conclusion

A key to building a business for the long term and being a succession thinker is to invest in leadership. There are two forms of leadership role that are critical in an SME: the organisation leader and the team leader. The organisation leader is a member of the organisation leadership team. That team has the mandate to deliver the vision. Developing the skills to do this is a long-term pursuit.

In an SME, we need to learn on the job and do the shared learning with our teammates. In building a team of leaders who are all responsible for the total business or the total system, you are building with an antifragile mindset. If any member of the team needs time off or has a life event, the others can lead the business. The business comprises a set of teams. A team leader has specific thematic accountabilities and then general team effectiveness accountabilities.

You may need to bring in team leaders for pragmatic reasons. Getting clarity on your Business Way will assist you to induct and train them to be successful. By building the capabilities of team leadership, you can percolate leaders.

You may feel like this is a lot to do. The key is patience, and to take the first step to recognise your role as an organisation leader, independent of your other roles.

It's common for Owner-Leaders to diagnose a problem and move to a solution with speed. It is wise to slow this and invest more time in diagnosing the problem. In doing this, you are leaning into an organisation leader's skill:

- Develop some habits so you can invest in your organisation's leadership roles.
- Allocate some part of the week to build organisation leadership skills – from trust building to systems thinking and sense making. Completing the activities throughout this book is a good start.

In the next chapter, we will explore how to build a culture beyond you. Many people join the business because of you. Your values are prevalent in the business even if they're not written. Moving a culture from implicit to explicit is critical to building a business beyond the current Owner-Leaders. To build a long-term business, you need to have aligned and productive people. We will now explore how to attract and retain such people.

# Chapter 6
# PRINCIPLE 4:
# BUILD CULTURE BEYOND YOU

## Introduction

Building and maintaining a healthy culture supports building a resilient business that can create value for the long term. A healthy company culture provides an environment to attract great and aligned people. Engaged and productive people who will care for your customers.

My discovery was that I enjoy collaborating with highly accountable people. This had a big effect on the values that were present in businesses I founded. As an SME Owner-Leader, you may find it difficult to attract people to your business because the salary market is hot. However, consciousness of your culture can be the place to differentiate yourself. In Daniel Pink's book *Drive*, he states people are motivated by three things: autonomy, mastery and connection to purpose. Moving from extrinsic motivation to intrinsic motivation mindsets for how to attract people is a good place to start. You have the decision rights to build your business to attract aligned and intrinsically motivated people.

The guidance for your culture begins with your owners' vision. This then informs your purpose and your values. The values are an important part of affecting behaviour, symbols and systems. Values can provide an accessible way to support decision making in the teams. The owners' value seeds form the basis upon which the values are grown. In many larger organisations, it is difficult to find the source of the values. In an SME, they come from the Owner-Leaders.

Each of the employees who joins your business goes on a journey, which I call the 'team member journey'. It is defined by the three Es:

- Entry into your business.
- Engagement while in your business.
- Exit from the business.

Analysis of the team member journey will help you build and embed your culture.

My story about the events of 2008, when my fellow owners stated they had my back, was another input into learning about culture. I wanted to build a culture that had the backs of its people. You can build a culture where the business has the backs of its people, customers and you. In this chapter we look at the cultural leadership framework, which provides an approach to deliver on this intent.

SME Owner-Leaders can harness the advantages of having a small system. You have the decision rights to define your culture. There are no constraints, and this is a place to differentiate your business. The only limitation is your imagination. To be a succession thinker, you need to attract capable, aligned people who can contribute for the long term. You may not compete on salary in certain overheated markets, but you can be disruptive. You can hire for the long term.

In 2018, the owners of acQuire decided to sell our software business after 22 years of operation. The average tenure of our organisation leaders was 14 years. The average tenure of our team leaders was 9 years and the average tenure of our employees was 8.6 years. We had 100 employees. acQuire was in a niche market. However, it was recognised as being a global leader in that niche. At our 20-year anniversary party we had our founding customers present. The success we achieved at acQuire was because we attracted aligned and capable people for long periods of time.

In this chapter, we will explore the team member journey and how the construction of a values constitution can support that journey. I will also explain how the cultural leadership framework supports the team member journey.

## Creating and embedding a values constitution

Building a business that is based on your values is the starting point to building a healthy culture and embedding it in a values constitution. The integrated owners' vision will affect the values you want for your business. Getting to the core of what the owners value and capturing this in value seeds is essential. One of the greatest advantages of being an owner is creating the culture that you think will achieve your goals and aspirations. There is a plethora of Royal Commissions and whistleblower events that have taken place in recent years because of a lack of values clarity or the corruption of values.

As Owner-Leaders, you value things in the world and certain behaviours. These become the implicit culture of your business. Think about teams you've worked on where you enjoyed it and you were at your most productive. Your teammates were connected and aligned. By making these values explicit, you can embed them throughout your business to maximise alignment.

Alignment of values is the secret source of building a healthy culture. For instance, I recently supported a team to craft their values. The owner is a scientist. He is passionate about critical thinking and how it affects the professional ethics of his business. He does not want people in his team who do not appreciate critical thinking.

Building alignment does not produce groupthink unless this is a value. However, succession thinkers build for the long term and any owners pushing groupthink would likely be doomed. Diversity is essential to innovative cultures. If the owners want diversity of thought, make it a value.

The owners get to seed the values constitution, but the team crafts and contributes to the final product. The scaffold comes from the owners, but the contribution by the team reinforces alignment.

A constitution is defined as a body of fundamental principles or established precedents according to which a state or other organisation is acknowledged to be governed. I use the term *constitution* with great intention – it underscores the gravitas of the values and the importance to decision making.

For the successful handover of decision rights a values constitution is critical. The following is a list of tips for what we have learned works when building a values constitution:

- The owners should capture their value seeds. They write the value as a verb statement so that each individual can put 'I will' in front of the value; for example, the value is maximising trust, therefore, 'I will maximise trust'.
- The owners should write a few bullet points to describe each value seed.

- As an organisation, leaders should run a workshop and mix up teams; put administrators with salespeople, for instance. Get them to challenge and elaborate on each value.
- Organisation leaders should craft the final version based on all the feedback.

When crafting the values, be clear that the way they're written can be unique and may only have a context in your Business Way. This authenticity is critical. An example is ADAPT's Give a Shit (GAS) value. We aren't flippant in our use of expletives. However, the GAS factor is referenced a lot in our business.

### Give a shit (GAS)

Having a high GAS factor means we care and want to be part of the solution. We choose to set our community and society up for success. This means people over profit. We are actively engaged with our work, our customers, our stakeholders and our community.

Your values constitution will develop. The ownership of it will change as well. It is wise to do an annual review. However, like your owners' vision, it will change slowly and with good organisation leadership and wisdom.

Building an authentic values constitution is the first step in underwriting a culture beyond you. It will provide the foundation to support distributing decision making across your business. The owners' vision and the values constitution are two sets of guidance that provide the guardrails for your business.

An example of using a value to support a big decision took place at ADAPT in 2019. ADAPT had a customer in an early stage that was struggling to pay our invoices and we provided payment terms to this customer. We were in a startup phase ourselves and it was a big decision. We did this because their business provided a critical health service, and we wanted their business to thrive and took a long-term view. They repaid the debt, and the company has now been a customer for six years.

The GAS factor helped us make a hard decision. Do we continue to provide services and technology without payment, especially given our financial situation? A well-implemented values constitution helps you and teams in your business make moral decisions when the heat is on.

As with visioning, there have been many failed value projects in the corporate world. Values are worthless if they are not authentic and practised. In my experience, they can become central to decision making. Without them, your succession thinking approach will be compromised. If you aren't building trust across the business, you'll never be comfortable to hand over. It's not optional. It is essential.

### Activity: What do you value?

The question we are trying to answer here is, what do you value? Your values will be evident in your business even if you have not made them explicit. This activity is intended to raise more awareness about your values. The Above the Line/Below the line model can inform us here.

What behaviours in other people drive you above the line to be creative and energetic? In short, what floats your boat?

What behaviours in other people drive you below the line? What makes you angry, anxious or low energy? In short, what upsets you?

You may discover that the values you build are things that you also break from time to time. However, values are also aspirational, and you need to keep working on them.

When forming these, try to form a verb statement. For instance, if you like to be both productive and have some fun, that could be: *be productive while sharing a gag*. You can put 'I will' in front of this value and take ownership. My intention here is to use plain English, not corporate word bingo.

Put each value seed into the following structure.

| Verb statement | |
|---|---|
| Description | Questions to validate the value |

To download this activity go to: www.successionthinking.com/activities

## Building cultural leadership

Culture cannot be delegated to a department, such as human resources. Cultural leadership is a critical accountability of an organisation leader. One organisation leader may have a greater accountability to the implementation, but the entire team is accountable to building a healthy culture.

In chapter 5 I introduced systems thinking. Your business is complex, with a lot of interdependent parts. If you put great people in poor processes and architectures, you will get poor results. Thinking about the journey of any team member can help you understand more about the system's view of culture. You can also start with an end in mind and work back to maximise healthy outcomes when people leave your system. You can explore the question, 'How do we get high-integrity leavers?' Cultural leadership can answer this question.

As an organisation leader, you will achieve better results by acknowledging that people will exit your business for a myriad of reasons. Mostly, it will be to do with their aspirations and where they want to go. However, in some situations you have a person who does not fit and you will start the exit conversation. The aim is to make this as high integrity as possible.

You can operate using an extrinsic motivation model or an intrinsic motivation model. An extrinsic approach is oriented towards thinking about financial incentives. An intrinsic motivation model leads to supporting an employee on their journey through your business and beyond.

Cultural leadership is where you design solutions in service of an intrinsic motivation approach. Therefore, alignment with your value system is so important. If an employee is not aligned with your values, they will not be intrinsically motivated. The cultural leadership needs to affect the fundamental design of the business. Two things that are common in extrinsic motivation businesses are power hierarchies and lack of transparency. Flatter and more open businesses will better support an intrinsic approach.

---

*Two things that are common in extrinsic motivation businesses are power hierarchies and lack of transparency.*

---

Cultural leaders drive trust and psychological safety in the organisation. Leading the understanding of trust is a big topic and can be underestimated. The exploration of trust, including account-ability trust, will help.

In the early stages of a business, cultural leadership starts out as an accountability of the organisation leader. Maybe you, as Owner-Leader, are the only cultural leader. As you grow, there will be more team leaders in your business. A way for you to maintain the culture is to keep connected to each person via a culture catch up. The intention is that each cultural leader builds a high-trust relationship with the employees in their cohort. The best design is when a cultural leader is not involved in each employee's day-to-day work, so the cultural leader can be truly in service to the employee. In the next topic, I will elaborate more on the team member journey and how the cultural leader supports it.

### Cultural Leadership design

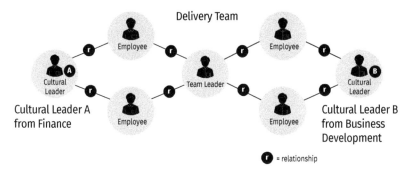

A cultural leader is not a counsellor. The role supports the team members' journey as they deliver in their roles. The cultural leader can be very supportive when life events happen to this team member. However, they can only problem solve within the walls of the business.

The cultural leadership framework has to be designed for the nuances of your business. As your business grows, the ratio of employees to organisation leaders will become too great. Therefore, the cultural leader framework needs to be redesigned. A potential design is for the organisation leaders' cohort to comprise team leaders. The team leaders then have cultural leader accountabilities to support the team members. This is shown in the following image.

A problem with distributing leadership is breaking the relationship with the recruiting Owner-Leader. An employee, hired by the founder, then has someone else as their team leader, so they may feel disconnected. This was a finding of the 'Exploring Distributed Leadership in the Small Business Context' paper. Cultural leadership is an approach to expanding team leadership while maintaining connection to the founder. These designs also fracture chain-of-command thinking and challenge power hierarchies.

In your business, it is wise to have two formal points of connection with employees. If the team leader is struggling, there is another point of connection to mitigate risk.

There is a cultural leader in every organisation. If it is not you, someone else will determine the culture. That is not necessarily your way. In his book *Drive*, Daniel Pink states that to believe people are incentivised by money alone is flawed, specifically as the cognitive demand of the job goes up. He asserts people are motivated by autonomy, mastery and purpose. Money is essential, but not at the cost of other drivers. My ADAPT colleagues and I have been tracking motivation in business for many years, and we have now built the measurement tools to do this in the ADAPT by Design platform. We have validated the findings in *Drive*. The key is to build a business that can attract the right people so you can deliver on your vision.

This was reinforced throughout my working life. However, an event in 2005 was the catalyst to the discovery of this for me. Steve enters my office and looks a little flat. Steve is a great member of our team. He is very good at his job – a Geoscience Data Analyst – and a good fit in our culture. The reason for his forlorn disposition was that he had come to tell me he wanted to take another job. This was very bad news for us. I could see that Steve was going to be a future leader of our business and it was going to be sad to see him go. I then asked some questions because I knew he was happy at acQuire. He said: 'They have offered me double my salary.' We were in the middle of a boom and companies were offering crazy (by this I mean non-sustainable) salaries. I had resigned to the idea that Steve was leaving because we could not compete with that salary. However, the next question changed everything: 'Where will you be working?' He said: 'It is an onsite, fly-in–fly-out position.' To me this made no sense. We were very supportive of Steve's athletic training (I call Steve an athlete because he went on to post a 2.48 marathon run). He did enviro challenges and a lot of running and kayak training. I could not see how this could be supported in a FIFO job. I put the following on the whiteboard (not quite as neat as it looks here).

| Category | Motivator | Job at acQuire | FIFO Job |
|---|---|---|---|
| Professional fit | 20 | 15 | 5 |
| Personal fit | 25 | 22 | 5 |
| Cultural fit | 20 | 18 | 5 |
| Training | 10 | 5 | 5 |
| Financial | 25 | 10 | 25 |
| TOTAL | 100 | 70 | 45 |

Scores are indicative only.

acQuire scored well in things that Steve values. Personal fit for instance. He could continue to do his training. We did increase Steve's salary but it was within our capability and a sustainable salary. Steve is still at the business today after traversing many roles. He did become the Leader of Product Development. This discovery led to the invention of the Job Satisfaction Calculator which was then renamed to the Career Valuation tool.

People want to work where they can develop mastery of their craft and where they are treated with respect and trusted. A place where they are not micromanaged and they can get more autonomy, and where they like the company and how it behaves. Purpose is where alignment comes into play. Your owner vision and your values are important in attracting aligned people.

The financial success of your people is essential, but this can be delivered by taking a long-term view of remuneration. Also, I recommend being the best employer when things are tough. Think about how you can build a future fund so you can keep your people through a downturn and be ready to go on the other side.

You might feel like this is a lot of work not directly related to current customer demand (it is), and be wondering, 'If I put a lot of time into this, will it pay off?' Answering this question drives an ROI versus ROV decision. Are you building for the short term or the long term? Putting time into this has a sustained payoff beyond you and your tenure. You are building infrastructure that will support growth and succession. Being a succession thinker will pay off.

## Developing the team member journey

Bringing your values to life and making sure they are not just a poster in the office is essential to underwriting your culture. If team members consistently experience behaviours and outcomes contrary to your values constitution, you have a big problem. It's better to have no values at all than to be disingenuous. Having aspirational, authentic values is essential. People will fall off the horse and break a value. When you, as an Owner-Leader, break a value, owning it in front of the team is critical.

To support your team to embed your company values, it is good to understand the team member journey and how the values can be embedded to support behaviour and decision making. Team members are the people critical to the success of your products and services – and they ultimately hold the customer relationships.

As the organisation leader, you are accountable for the team member journey. The team member journey is called the 'three Es'; **entry** into your business, **engagement** while in your business and **exit** from your business. It may appear harsh to discuss exit when our intention is to invest in people for the long run. However, starting with the end in mind helps the design of the team member journey. You want high-integrity leavers – people you would welcome back. To avoid having low-integrity leavers, you need to invest in a good design for team member entry and engagement.

To build for the long term you need team members who are in your business because they want to be there. You don't want financial hostages – people working there only because the pay is good – because that just won't last. Therefore, you should think about intrinsic motivation at each point of the team member journey. Motivation associated with each person's job can be broken into seven categories:

- Professional fit
- Personal fit
- Cultural fit
- Training
- Mentorship
- Feedback
- Financial.

Let's examine these categories.

| Motivation category | Typical questions | Motivation magnitude (%) | How are we doing? |
|---|---|---|---|
| *Professional fit* | How important is it for you to utilise your existing skills, experience and other professional attributes? | | |
| *Personal fit* | How important is it for you to live an integrated life where your engagement with friends and family, community recreation and work are balanced? | | |
| *Cultural fit* | How important is it for you to work at a company where values are not just defined but well embedded? | | |
| *Training* | How important is training and professional development to you? How important is it for you to have access to training to learn new skills and develop new talents? | | |
| *Mentorship* | How important is mentorship to you in your ideal role? | | |
| *Feedback* | How important is it for you to receive feedback from your peers and leaders for personal and professional growth? | | |
| *Financial* | How important is your base and variable salary package? | | |
| Total | | 100 | |

We call this decision tool a 'career valuation tool'. It helps to support the team member journey.

The extrinsic motivation assumption seems to be that salary and money are the only motivators for taking jobs. Companies will often advertise the financial package for a position, but rarely are other metrics provided. Some people are more motivated by money than others. However, often it is simply a 'time of life' motivation. If the person is 34 years old and just signed up for a mortgage, money goes up in their motivation. A 23-year-old who wants to accumulate knowledge in their craft may put a greater emphasis on company-supported training. Tracking motivation through the team member journey allows you to optimise your support of each team member.

A team member can be held to account on a team by their peers and the team leader. But a cultural leader can support the team member's journey through the business. They may end up on several teams and move at different times of their career, including moving to a job outside your business.

## Entry of a team member

To build for the long term, you need aligned people who can be effective contributors. Recruiting processes are often like a speed date. We don't invest enough in making the best decision for both parties. That is why in succession thinking, we consider the entry of team members to be a common point of failure. In having a team leader and a cultural leader support the recruiting process, we can mitigate some of the 'speed dating' risks.

For the team leader, daily demands can overwhelm the recruiting decision and poor outcomes can result. The science and art of recruiting is a subject of many books, and I do not want to explore that here.

However, there are some high-level risk-mitigation approaches that are important for you as an Owner-Leader of an SME.

The costs of a failed hire are large. The challenges caused by having a non-aligned team member will be disruptive. Having two separate interviews mitigates risk when hiring. The team leader does the analysis of skills fit and the cultural leader does the analysis of cultural fit.

The cultural leader can use a career valuation approach to interview a prospective team member using the following process:

- Capture their motivation percentages – ask them to distribute 100 points across the seven motivations categories.
- Ask the candidate to rate their previous job against the motivation categories. Where there are big differences, understand what is behind the dissatisfaction. For instance, if training is 15% of their motivation and they gave it 2 at their old job, that means there's a differential of 13. The candidate was dissatisfied with how they were being supported in training. This provides the basis for a quality conversation. (It might show that there would be no improvement in your business. Often you will help them make more sense of why they left their previous job.)

In doing this, the cultural leader will get good insights and determine if the prospective team member will have the same issues in your business. The cultural leader shares the values constitution as part of this interview and assesses the candidate's alignment. In your recruitment process, you may also have the concept of a 'simulation', where fellow team members can be involved to assess the membership of the team. The two leaders would also take part and, with the other data, be able to make an informed decision.

## Engagement of a team member

At an interval that makes sense, the cultural leader can catch up with the team member and check in using the career valuation approach. The intention is to capture feedback about the differences between their motivations and what they can achieve in your business. They will also receive feedback about their contribution from the team leader and their teammates. But the catchup is for the cultural leader to capture the feedback to optimise the team member journey.

In the same way a customer gives feedback on your product, the team member is giving feedback to improve their connection to the business. The cultural leader facilitates the process, as follows:

- Capture their motivations. Motivations change depending on life events and the phase of life. The opportunity cost model helps people to think more about what they actually want, not just to optimise for financial return. It introduces a longer term approach and drives a conversation about the team member's ROV.
- Beginning with the categories that have the highest weighting, ask how well your business can meet these desires. You are asking this to get real feedback, so the person has to feel safe. You are trying to work out what is missing and fix it.
- Analyse the categories that have high weighting and a low feedback score. Explore why and assess what can be done about closing the gap. This may require you doing some research to see whether you *can* close the gap. Sometimes you will not have a solution and this may be the beginning of a high-integrity exit decided by the team member.
- When you do the cultural fit, discuss the values constitution. Have a conversation about each value and then ask if we – the

company – are living it. Ask what more we can do to assist with using the values in decision making.

- This activity is done for the entire time that a team member is in your business. This is their team member journey. If the data is recorded, you have the history, which in itself creates a healthy conversation.

## Exit of a team member

If the person has been engaged on their team member journey by their team leader and cultural leader, you increase the probability of a high-integrity exit. High integrity means that the team member did not need to deceive you or their team members – they could be open about their desire to go to another role outside the business. They felt safe to be open. The leaders did everything to maximise trust and psychological safety for the team member.

In 2013, I met with Stephen. He was an ex-member of acQuire and had taken a job with a company in New Zealand. When he left acQuire, we had many conversations about whether he should take this new role. It was a high-integrity exit. Stephen had left acQuire in 2011 after working there for six years, and worked in his new role in the New Zealand company for two years. Stephen was keen to reenter acQuire.

Although I was an owner, I had handed over my organisation leader roles. The leadership team supported Stephen's reentry, and Steven is still there as of January 2023. Investment in the team member journey maximises high-integrity exits from your business and enables reentry of people who are highly effective and well aligned.

## Why focus on the team member journey?

The following I-We-It model, created by Doug Stone and Sheila Heen from the Harvard Negotiation Project, has many applications for making sense of your business. I will use it here to help explain why the team member journey is critical to you as an Owner-Leader building for the long term. The 'I' represents you. 'We' represents your team. 'It' represents the customer and the marketplace.

The following diagram shows, as your business evolves, you start with all your focus on the 'It'. You are critical to understanding the market, sales and delivery of your products and services. As you grow, your focus needs to rotate to the 'We', the team. The 'We' will evolve to take accountability for the 'It'. The dotted arrows show your journey from 'It' to 'We' – the development of the organisation leader's role. The grey arrow shows the 'We'. The team develops the accountability for the 'It'. They're looking after operations. Therefore, the team member journey is as important to you as the customer journey. As time progresses, they are accountable for the customer journey.

You may have invested in people that you felt let you down. They left your business after you'd made a significant contribution

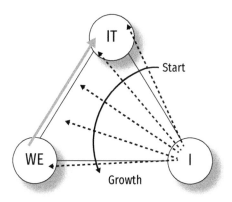

to them, and it hurt. You might be thinking, 'This looks like a lot of effort – I have no guarantee this will work and I don't want to be let down again.' But to build for the long term, I do not believe there is an alternative. People will come and go, and the societal trend of high mobility may become even more prevalent. However, you'll be able to compete favourably in all economic circumstances when you are searching for people. This is an area where you want to be able to differentiate yourself. The ROV investment does pay off.

## Conclusion

In this chapter, you were introduced to ideas for building culture beyond you. These ideas help build a healthy and highly differentiated workplace. You will create the conditions for distributed decision making because the values constitution will be embedded.

This is critical for you as an Owner-Leader. You can't hand over without being able to trust the system, not just the people. Build culture as a system. It can persist as people change. Your culture needs continuous support and monitoring.

With the establishment of cultural leadership, you are putting accountability in place to maintain the culture you want. You are not leaving it to chance. By developing a team member journey, you can embed your values constitution throughout entry, engagement and exit.

A term that has become common is to be an 'employer of choice'. It may be a cliche, but you want to build a place that attracts effective and aligned people who can contribute for the long term. Even if some members only stay for shorter periods, you will maximise their effectiveness while in your team.

Some traditional advice from HR is to build on a scarcity model for people. This is driven by fear and potential legal ramifications. You do need to adhere to all legal requirements of your jurisdiction, but fear-based HR is a race to the bottom. As a succession thinker, it is wise to invest in an abundant mindset about people. I acknowledge this does not mean people will always do well by you. However, I recommend using your creativity to differentiate yourself and design a team member journey truly aligned to your values.

I've been referencing your Business Way throughout the book. In the next chapter we explore the content of your Business Way and introduce a data-driven mindset for its management.

## Chapter 7

# PRINCIPLE 5:
# BUILD YOUR BUSINESS WAY

## Introduction

Your Business Way will be maintained by all team members, and empowers succession for all in the business. Your Owner-Director team provides the integrated owners' vision as a root or starting point. Your Business Way custodians are the owner, director and organisation leadership teams, and its upkeep is done by all teams.

Your Business Way is a set of data for Owner-Leaders that is the tangible product of succession thinking. It is data that must not be confused with operations-based technologies and data systems. In the same way that your accountants use Xero, MYOB or NetSuite (to name a few) to manage financial transactions, Owner-Leaders can manage the data that holds your Business Way.

The data will be there in perpetuity and outlast any specific leader or team member. This data may exist in a variety of places, including documents on the file system and in a set of technologies. Being able to integrate and relate this data is highly valuable.

The idea of having data for Owner-Leaders to describe your business may be novel to you. Most SME Owner-Leaders spend their time in operations, so you may have built a good set of technologies to support operations-based data. But as an Owner-Leader you need systems that support building for the long term and can support the interdependence of things.

Given the nature of this data and how it relates across the business, it can be difficult to set up, manage and maintain. Exploring the problem of storing this in a form it can be used by your organisation is a challenge. As explained in chapter 2, ADAPT by Design has built a technology to house Business Ways. In this chapter, I will focus on the data and the underserved need, not on our technology. However, for convenience I will use examples that are produced using our technology.

Some of your Business Way is data that will evolve in perpetuity. Your business is complex, and you want to make this as simple as possible for all your stakeholders. Capturing your Business Way in an accessible form that can be maintained as part of the operations of business is the objective. Its upkeep is distributed across the business and not centralised. However, the custodians are the Owner-Director and the Organisation Leadership Team.

---

*Your business is complex, and you want to make this as simple as possible for all your stakeholders. Capturing your Business Way in an accessible form that can be maintained as part of the operations of business is the objective.*

---

To understand the connection to Owner-Leaders' data, let's go back to my origins in acQuire, the resources software company we started in 1996. We discovered that the original observations and measurements collected as data to support financial and safety decisions in the resources industry were poor quality. This drove the development of our products and services. The building of acQuire's data management products supported our education about data, and led me to ask: where do we store the observations and measurements that define our way of doing things? It took a long time to answer this question, and it was not fully answered until ADAPT by Design was founded.

As a succession thinking leader, you need a place to store your Business Way so you can provide clarity and support to current and future stakeholders of your business. This will support leaders to build a resilient and adaptive business. It also supports the clarity and delivery of the vision.

The concept was not the result of an epiphany – a set of problems that accumulated over a long period drove us to this development. A core discovery was made when I was at a point where I had handed over all operational roles. We had 100-plus people distributed across seven offices in six countries. The documentation of position descriptions and clarity of accountability for each employee was poor. We would do a massive documentation run each year to regenerate the agreement for each employee. At the time, our clarity about positions and roles for employees was still evolving. We really struggled with the adaptation of position descriptions as people's work evolved in our business. We would change how we engaged the customer or add a new product and our documentation was immediately out of date. We needed to connect changes in the way we did business to roles and teams. An individual's role stack can evolve as a function of the development of the business. Although we were very unclear where this would take us, we started to see the data interdependence problem.

An important point to make here is about your Business Way being described in data. I have not found much in my research about this concept. There are a lot of case studies about what specific companies have done in this area; however, there is not much about the idea of abstracting it to the general case. Also, the underserved need of a succession thinking Owner-Leader, building for the long term, is very different. We can describe this data because as much as SMEs are complex, the total system is more visible and at the simple end of complexity. By bringing your Business Way to life, you can build what Peter Senge in *The Fifth Discipline* calls a 'learning organisation'.

In chapter 2, we defined your Business Way and what contributes to it. In this chapter, we are going to explore the data sets that make up your Business Way.

## The Business Way components

I have defined the purpose of your Business Way, but I have not gone into the details yet. So let's explore the data that makes up your business way.

**Business Way**

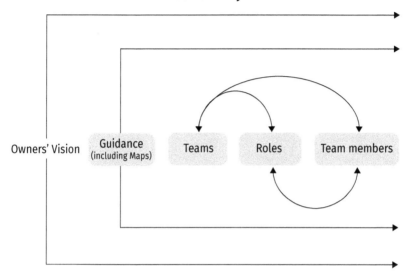

Your Business Way consists of:

**A set of guidance:**

- Integrated internal vision (the root)
- External vision
- Purpose
- Values constitution
- Markets/Product and services (economic engine guidance)
- Goals and objectives
- Measurement of progress on goals and objectives
- Organisation maps
- Customer flow maps

**A set of teams:**

- Customer flow teams
- Support teams

- Stewardship teams:
  - Owner-Director
  - Organisation Leader

A set of roles that are related to those teams for example:

**Owner-Director team roles:**

- Owner
- Director

**A set of team data:**

- team members that have roles on teams
- teams that have systems to describe the work they do.

This schema describes your Business Way. It is persistent from SME to SME, but the content will be vastly different. The challenge for us as SME Owner-Leaders is that our schema is not static. It is changing all the time. How can we manage the challenge of having the *best approximation* of our business at any time? How do we develop an approach so that the dynamic nature is distributed to all, not centralised as an onerous and difficult task?

The stewards of your Business Way are the Owner-Directors and Organisation Leadership Team. The objective is that all teams take ownership of their part so your Business Way evolves. This is why team leadership is so important in succession thinking.

Your Business Way is where all roles are held, and any succession event requires the handover of a role. It is a set of data made up of guidance, teams, roles, systems and team members. This data is interdependent and dynamic. SME Owner-Leaders who harness this data can enhance business performance in the short term, but just as importantly can contribute to sustained value creation.

The idea that you can only ever understand an approximation of your Business Way is important. It is very liberating, and connects better with an entrepreneurial understanding of the business.

I acknowledge this is a challenging concept when you first explore it. However, you are already doing most of this. I'm suggesting the unifying concept of your Business Way as a means to support succession thinking.

---

*SME Owner-Leaders who harness this data can enhance business performance in the short term, but just as importantly can contribute to sustained value creation.*

---

## Your Business Way: Guidance

In my experience, there have been many effective strategy formation events where only parts of the good thinking made it off the butcher's paper. You may not think of the output of these workshop days as a set of interdependent guidance essential to the direction of the business. But guidance captured in the right form can be used to inform meaningful progress.[6] You may have found it difficult to make this information available to all the people in your business in a convenient way. It might be in a PDF or in a set of slides, but it is not easily available to all. You may have found you have different versions that cause confusion.

The following table shows some of the data that contributes to your Business Way.

---

6    See Business Way schema.

**Business Way**

| Owners Vision | | |
|---|---|---|
| **Guidance** | **Teams** | **Team Members** |
| Vision statement | Team guidance. Purpose of team and clarity of accountability. | Measures to support team member journey |
| Purpose | Measures of team effectiveness including trust and psychological safety | Manage role clarity and how roles connect to teams. |
| Values constitution | Support for effective stewardship. Support for effective meetings, tracking or work and decision making. | |
| Market guidance (Products & services) | Storage and management of team systems – how the team works. | |
| Goals & objectives | Clarity of roles that collectively deliver the team's purpose. | |
| Measurement of progress on goals | | |
| Organisation maps (How are teams organised?) | | |
| Customer flow maps | | |
| Measurement of organisation effectiveness. How to improve. | | |

It is rare that content like this is thought of as data, but if you're going to build culture beyond you, your values constitution becomes critical data. Providing a place to store the core truth for all your guidance assists with clarity and comprehension. In chapter 5, I stated that sense-making is an important skill of an organisation leader. Providing the environment so any team member can obtain this information on demand is essential. The alternative of pushing information to people at a time that is not convenient to them tends to be an unsatisfactory means of communication. By treating information of this type with a data mindset, you can also start to consider the semantics associated with how to describe the information. How could you store a value (part of your values constitution), for instance?

Another set of information that is often not digitised in a form for leading is your business goals and objectives. A popular approach that we recommend is the objectives and key results model, founded by Andy Grove at Intel. To be able to integrate this data into the total guidance system for your business is powerful. This can provide an effective way to make sure strategy is implemented and make it visible to all.

In succession thinking an organisation leader is always aware of the total system integrated with the intrinsic motivation of the team members. The more context you can give people the more they can contribute. Also, you can design to maximise productivity while solving for team autonomy. Organisation maps are a way of doing this, and can be thought of as the next generation to an organisation chart.

You need to provide some clarity on where your customer flow teams, support teams and stewardship teams sit. The organisation map provides a place to make sense of this. The above diagram shows the idea that our customer teams are part of our economic engine and our support and stewardship teams are there to form a foundation upon which the economic engine can deliver.

Another form of mapping in greater detail is customer flow mapping. This is a topic too large for this book. However, these maps are a critical part of the guidance of your Business Way. You are probably already building these maps but they are not thought of as interdependent on

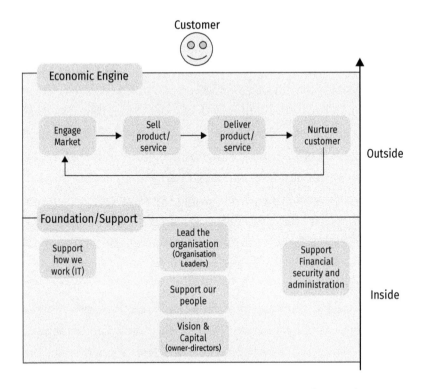

other components of your Business Way. Most professional services businesses have a similar high-level critical customer flow. To help with explanation I will use verbs to name the teams. Engage market > Sell offering > Deliver offering > Nurture customers. The critical customer flow can be constructed at different levels of detail. However, these four teams interoperate to deliver your products and services.

Guidance, including maps, is informed by sense-making. Deborah Ancona, a professor at MIT Sloan School of Business, wrote an essay on sense-making: 'Sensemaking: Framing and acting in the unknown'. I have paraphrased a story about a group of Italian troops lost in the Swiss Alps. They were tired, hungry and worried. One of the soldiers found a map in his backpack. They used this map as a guide, but they then realised that the map was for the Pyrenees, not the Swiss Alps. The key message we can apply from this to your Business Way is it's better to have something that is partially written than nothing at all. I often refer to the 62% rule because the 80% rule is too ambitious. Cut a version, deploy it, get feedback and cut another version. It is okay for it to be imperfect because it never will be perfect. It will always be an approximation.

## Your Business Way: Teams

Throughout this topic I will elaborate on how teams fit into your Business Way data. Here are some team characteristics you must understand:

- The building blocks of your business are teams made up of members who execute specific roles.
- Your business delivers its products and services to customers using teams that are part of the customer flow.
- Your business runs by getting support from a range of teams and these grow as the business grows. Often you will have finance, people and culture or business systems teams. This group is called the support teams.
- Two teams that have been the focus of this book and are critical to succession thinking are the Owner-Director and Organisation Leadership Team. This group can be called the stewardship teams.

How these teams relate to each other is important. Being able to optimise accountability and ultimately productivity is vital. In chapter 5, I underscored the importance of developing good team leaders. A core attribute of an effective team is role clarity. People are on the team to execute a role. For instance, the delivery team has a role called 'implementer', and Alice is a team member in this role. Relating the team role and Alice is important as part of describing your Business Way. The role description will be important to Alice in understanding how to contribute. The team has many 'how do we … ?' questions, and the answers for these are coded in what we call 'systems'. This is where you capture vital information about how you work. Systems have many benefits, including training of new team members, handover of roles and alignment of team members.

In chapter 5 we discussed the topic of distributed leadership. Distributing decision rights to teams to update how they work supports the upkeep of your Business Way. It will never be perfect but it will be a close approximation. This is a powerful concept, however it needs team leaders to care about continuously capturing how you work. This is essential to long-term businesses, but you also get immediate benefits on your next hire. It improves induction and training significantly.

Teams are a building block of business. In succession thinking we need to understand the relationship between teams, roles, team members and systems. We also need to develop the knowledge of how each team interoperates with other teams.

A story that may help consolidate understanding here came in 2011. I had been out of operations for two years and as an organisation leader was supporting the design work for architecting acQuire, including the systemisation of how we worked. We had been using a technology call Blueworks to capture role-based workflow. As a technology company we had the internal resources to write our own code to solve interoperability challenges. We got the idea of integrating Active Directory (our people) with role-based workflow. This was a founding experiment that led to thinking about integrating the data described in the schema. As with a lot of discoveries there was no great epiphany, just lots of little experiments. This was one of the contributing discoveries that led to the genesis of the adapt platform – now called adapt HQ.

You might have teams in your business but they are a loose grouping of people, or you might think of teams as a group of people independent of roles. You might even think, 'I will hire smart people and they will work it out.' This is sound thinking in one way, but only while the current team is together.

Your business may be in a period of high performance and the people you have on board are exceptional. I congratulate you on this. However, it does not mean your business has been built for succession or is resilient.

## Your Business Way: Team members

Here is an aspirational story about Alice, a team member in your business. Imagine you have built your Business Way with succession thinking.

### Team components and Alice

Alice sits on the delivery team in the role of implementer. She also has other roles because she sits on a product team. The delivery team has a particular purpose to execute on a set of accountabilities, documented and understood by the team. The delivery leader has been trained in your Business Way and gives Alice context so she can be effective. The systemisation used by the delivery team is built and supported by the team, but also dovetails with other teams' inter-actions. By having the systemisation distributed, the whole team can participate in its innovation on an as-needed basis.

## Guidance components and Alice

Alice will make decisions both in her role and as part of the team. The vision, purpose and values constitution will support that decision making. Alice will have interactions with other team members, both on this team and on other teams. The behaviours that support these interactions will support Alice's alignment to your culture. The delivery team can deliver to the strategy set by the organisation leaders because it is transparent and implementable. The delivery team is part of the customer flow, and Alice understands this flow so she can give feedback for its improvement beyond her own team. Access to sense-making maps helps her improve the business.

## Team member components: Alice as a team member

Alice's ability to make a positive impact is affected by:

- her acumen to execute the role
- her motivation
- the team leader's capability to support the attributes of an effective team.

Alice has cultural data that supports her team member journey from entry and engagement to exit, with the objective of high integrity.

Alice has the opportunity to master her craft, and she has cultural catchups so she and her cultural leader can discuss how the business is aligned to her current wants and needs. Alice receives feedback from her delivery leader and her peers about where she can improve her contribution. She is in a high-trust environment, and has autonomy to get on with it and not be micromanaged. She is in a culture where she is respected.

In this aspirational story, there are a variety of outcomes that have a positive impact on your business:

- Alice is on a number of teams and is less effective in one of those roles.
- The role clarity allows her to hand over to a successor.
- Although life events can impact everyone, Alice has no reason to move and every reason to stay.
- Alice has a lot of influence in the industry she works in and recommends your business as a fantastic place to work.
- Your customers like that Alice is both good at her job and is supported well by the company to execute effectively.
- Your customers are sticky; they are long-term customers because of the quality of the service Alice delivers.
- Alice wants to be a team leader. You think she has the attributes and skills to deliver, and you can be clear what it means to be a team leader in your Business Way.
- She is in a good position to hand over her role because of its clarity. She wants to stay in the business and so will be available to train her successor.
- The organisation leadership team over recent years has contributed to this cumulative story of building your Business Way. Alice is a potential successor for the organisation leadership team.

Imagine that Alice's story holds for all members of your business. Your Business Way is led by the organisation leaders, but nurtured by all. Alice's story highlights the interdependence that is so central to your Business Way.

You might think that this seems too aspirational, or you feel you are well on the way to achieving this. If it's the latter, well done. However, if you think it is too aspirational, it might be because you feel you have to solve this by next Tuesday. I've been doing this for more than 20 years in two companies. It's a decision to adopt succession thinking and lean into the principles. Let this develop over time.

## Conclusion

Your Business Way is made up of interdependent components, a set of guidance, a set of teams, a set of roles related to those teams, a set of team data. All of this data can be considered as part of your Business Way.

Your Business Way is a set of Owner-Leader data that will evolve in perpetuity, and you want to make it as simple as possible for all your stakeholders. Capturing your Business Way in an accessible form means that it can be maintained as part of the operations of the business. Its upkeep is distributed across the business and not centralised. The big prize for you in capturing your Business Way is that it supports all the succession thinking principles.

The development of your Business Way improves induction training and ultimately the excellence of your business, but it's also the baton to pass over time. Your Business Way is the continuum across different leaders. Given that it is described by dynamic data, the management of it is well served by software solutions. The interdependence and dynamic nature of the components and the need for decentralisation of its upkeep supports the biological nature of your business.

Historically, businesses were built by setting up departments that were constructed as independent parts. To manage accountability there was often a hierarchical organisational chart. Many of these areas evolved because of the size of the organisation. You're an SME Owner-Leader and can harness your advantage: your systems are complex, but at the simple end because of decision rights and size.

The road to excellence is to treat your business like a piece of software. Cut a version and then get feedback so it can improve. All your team members have different pictures of how your business works. Help align people on the assumption they are not playing the same video. Invest in the ideas of sense-making to support doing this.

---

*The road to excellence is to treat your business like a piece of software. Cut a version and then get feedback so it can improve.*

---

Now that you've been introduced to all five principles, in the next chapter let me show you how you can understand them in more detail by exploring a case study: my own succession journey in ADAPT by Design.

# Chapter 8
# SUCCESSION THINKING: A CASE STUDY

## Introduction

To help you activate succession thinking in your business, I will share the ups and downs of my application of these principles. I will share my story from founding ADAPT by Design (now adapt) to being an active owner of adapt. All of my other roles have been handed over. I'm sharing my journey because I can share a greater level of detail and it would have asked a lot of our customer colleagues to share this level of transparency.

adapt was founded to take succession thinking solutions to SME Owner-Leaders. Our purpose has been to help SME Owner-Leaders build resilient businesses. At its founding in 2014, our knowledge of succession thinking was based on my experience in founding acQuire and the experience of succession there. We have since learnt a great deal by engaging the market and working with other Owner-Leaders.

The principles shared in this book would not have been written this way in 2014. For instance, in 2014 succession thinking was called 'total system succession'. Instead of the five principles outlined here, I would speak about eight 'successions'. Although the methods of communicating it and making it accessible have evolved significantly, the core tenets have persisted.

Within this case study, I will use the current principles as a way of explaining how adapt has been stewarded by succession thinking and how it has supported my own succession aspirations. I wanted to build a resilient business that can deliver for the long term. My customers are building for the long term, so it is essential we are here to support them for the long term too. In sharing this case study, I will explore each principle in the period between July 2020 and my final handover that was completed on 23 December 2022. I've explored the journey through the lens of the principles, so it is not chronological. The capacity to do the final handovers was based on work done five years prior. By explaining my own succession out of adapt using the five principles, these principles become more accessible.

## Principle 1: Seek role clarity

Given I am the founder of adapt, I had every type of role: owner, director, organisation leader, team leader and principal technician. In June 2020, all of the roles I performed were documented (in a basic form) as part of the adapt Way. I had many of the pains and challenges that other SME Owner-Leaders had. A big challenge for me was the relationship between my vision for the business and the capital available to go after it. We were – and are – trying to do a big thing with limited capital. During the 2020 annual offsite meeting,

I shared with my teammates that as a 59-year-old startup entrepreneur, I was tired and understood that it was going to take more time and energy to deliver the vision.

We agreed that we needed to deal with my full role stack succession. I had handed over the majority of my product roles and some of my team leadership roles. However, I still had roles on customer teams and was the team leader of the organisation leadership team. The succession for these roles could not be found inside the business.

We documented our annual objectives that captured the challenge and drove us to find a solution. The objective was formed in July 2020. These objectives (see below) were visible to the whole business. My succession was totally transparent. However, I had to helicopter in a leader because I could not percolate one. The person was not going to learn the adapt Way over time. Given this, I designed more risk mitigation into my succession solution.

I was looking for an entrepreneurial successor. I wanted to find an entrepreneur keen to build over the next 10 to 15 years. Therefore, I had succession of ownership linked with the succession of other roles. Given I wanted to attract a highly aligned person who was prepared to put in capital, I needed to merge a recruitment process with a mergers acquisition process and build towards an integrated owners' vision that we could both sign off on.

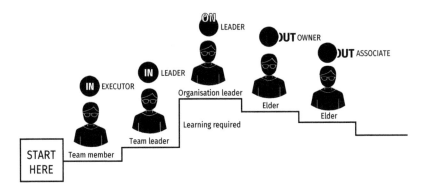

Imagine if I had not built ADAPT by Design with role clarity. What would I have handed over and how? The acumen required to execute each role was clear and defined in each role. I could not hand over these roles internally and had to mitigate the risks of a helicopter leader. I was looking for a co–Owner-Director as well as someone who could execute the leadership and technician roles. Without succession thinking, I would not have had the infrastructure in place to execute this complex succession.

## Principle 2: Build your owners' vision

Of the five principles, this was my last discovery. I documented this as the second principle but found it late. This came from working with other SME Owner-Leaders and seeing that my own vision was not well articulated. I was complicating my market vision with my owner vision. This created a lot of difficulty for the people inside ADAPT by Design. We were building an offering that required the development of software products. We needed a significant amount of capital, and I was the only supplier. We were consequently under-resourced for the offering we wanted to build. My vision for the business meant I could not take ROI capital – I needed to find ROV capital. In the process of finding an Owner-Leader successor, I did more work on my owner vision to support the analysis of alignment.

I built an information memorandum. This allowed any candidate to do due diligence early in the process. The information memorandum was a PDF with URLs leading into the platform that stored the adapt Way.

In December 2020, I met Gabe Enslin at a cafe in Subiaco. Many years previously I read a book called *Blink* by Malcom Gladwell. He talks about gut instincts and thin slicing. How in a small window of time you seem to be able to make decisions based on intuition. My first meeting with Gabe was one of these experiences. I kicked of the chat saying that I was having a few issues supporting my wife, Debbie. The support issue related to the COVID check-in app on her iPhone. Gabe said: 'You know what my current role is don't you?' I said that I did at a high level. He said, 'The company I work for wrote that app and I lead the support team.' He said, 'Give me Debbie's number and I will get it fixed.' Gabe subsequently fixed Debbie's phone issue. Her feedback to me confirmed my intuition that Gabe looks like a good fit to continue the founding of adapt.

This was the first round of many meetings and workshops to discuss our alignment. (I will discuss the recruitment and handover of roles later in this chapter.) The process with respect to ownership alignment was to sign a mutual letter of intent. This made it clear what we agreed to until the next decision gate in October of that year. We then signed an implementation agreement that took us through to ultimately signing a shareholders' agreement.

Gabe and I were entering a business marriage. Gabe was not coming in to lead an established business; he was going to continue the founding process. I don't know what you call this but perhaps it is a Continuity Founder or a Co-Founder. There is no greater risk than to go into a business marriage on hope alone. Alignment is everything. How do you mitigate the risk of non-alignment in timeframes that aren't glacial? I had learned that not having my owner vision clear to all my stakeholders created angst. What would happen if this was not clear with someone who now has the decision rights to change the vision? At the pessimistic end, it would maximise the probability of a high-integrity business divorce. At the optimistic end, you would find great alignment and build an abundant outcome together.

The shareholders' agreement was signed at the beginning of 2023. The shareholders' agreement has evolved to support our integrated owners' vision. Gabe is now an active Owner-Leader and is on the organisation leadership team as a vision custodian and Leader of adapt. A small but I think important thing to consider here is the brand associated with titles. It is my view that the C-Suite is a PLC concept. The CEO brand has been damaged due to stories of massive salaries and golden parachutes. Given Owner-Leaders often eat last (not first), it is my belief that Owner-Leaders do themselves an injustice using this title.

## Principle 3: Build leadership beyond you

I want to make it clear that I made a lot of errors here, especially in the first half of ADAPT by Design's journey. I'm not talking about people failing or not wanting to deliver a quality solution. I made impatient succession decisions. I was a succession thinker in training.

Succession thinking is about building infrastructure. I, and the team, learned a lot which contributed to innovations in our succession thinking offerings. There were a number of issues, but the common problem was underestimating the learning journey required to become an organisation leader. At the time, we started looking for my Owner-Leader successor. We were starting to build good practices in which our organisation leadership capability evolved. The clarity of structure and practices of the organisation leadership team were critical to initiating this succession.

Building antifragile leadership, as discussed in chapter 5, is key to being able to hand over something you really care about. I wanted an active Owner-Leader on this team, but I also wanted a team that can run well if Gabe has a life event such as a sickness. The half-life of my knowledge of the business landscape depreciates with speed, and even six months after handover I would struggle to be relevant. I could support the team to do the work but not reenter the role.

For Gabe to enter into the business, we went through multiple interviews that began with me and included my Owner-Director advisers, David Stephen and Suzanne McGrechan. This included a simulation where he participated with the leadership team to navigate a big go-to-market challenge.

We agreed that in the first four months, Gabe had to give us confidence that he was able to be an organisation leader in the sell function, execute as a shared value (a technician) lead on the sell team and deliver as a resilient business coach (a technician) on the delivery team.

In hindsight, this was asking a lot of Gabe. However, we wanted to see his acumen. He did not have to be a gun on all skills at this stage. In October, after the four-month trial, we signed an implementation agreement, which included clarity in building a full succession map that was visible to everyone in the business. This showed when every role I had was going to be transitioned to Gabe or other role recipients.

### The handover plan

| | Organisation Leader | Team Leader | Technician / Team Member | Ownership |
|---|---|---|---|---|
| 1st December 2021 | Lead adapt | | Method Designer | |
| | Primary phase | | | |
| | Support our people Leader | | | |
| February 2022 | Support our people Leader | Team Leader of Navigation (OLT) | | |
| | Tertiary phase | | | |
| July 2022 | Lead adapt | | Shared Value lead | |
| | | | Shared Value lead | |
| January 2023 | | | Resilient Business Coach | GABE Joins as Owner Director |
| June 2023 | | | Resilient Business Coach | |

There were still errors made, and this did not mitigate all issues. There was some cultural turbulence that I will talk about soon. In short, the succession event triggered people to reassess their aspirations.

A key to my comfort with succession is the transparency of data to me. The following data tells me the effectiveness of the organisation's leaders as measured by each team member.

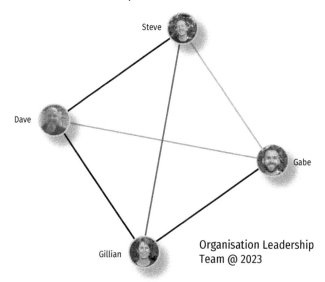

Organisation Leadership
Team @ 2023

**Team scores of the organisation leadership team – January 2023**

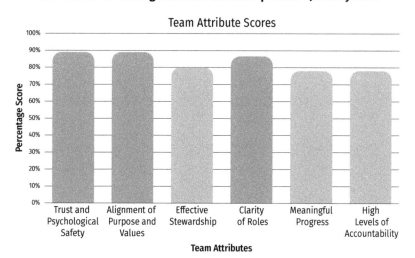

Prior to my own succession beginning, we had built good organisation leadership practices. This had been driven by trying to distribute leadership from the beginning. It took time and we had the problem of me trying to hand over too fast. However, we eventually built a solid organisation leadership team that created the base to induct a new member. We could not percolate a leader over time. We consequently had to do some thinking about how to hire from the outside and mitigate the risk.

## Principle 4: Build culture beyond you

As the Owner-Leader, I seeded our values constitution in 2014. Many of these values came across from acQuire. The values have since been updated and are displayed below.

Values Constitution >

Maximise Trust

Grow Together

Give a Shit – GAS

Build Shared Value

Walk the ADAPT Way

If you cross reference these with our owners' vision, you can see that they align and give people a decision-making framework. Each of these values is described in more detail to make this possible.

**Build Shared Value**

Our Meaning

ADAPTers are purpose people, actively helping to build the society in which we want to live. We create value so it maximises outcomes for all stakeholders, our people, our customers, our society and our environment. We recognise our success and social progress are interdependent.

Ask Yourself

Do we give our customers and stakeholder more than we take?

Am I contributing to building a strong SME community?

Do I ensure ADAPT is fairly recognised for the value we provide?

The cultural leadership team has been operating since the start of the business. The organisation leaders have broken this out as a separate role and each organisation leader supports a small number of team members.

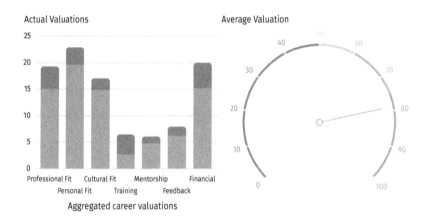

Aggregated career valuations

The aggregation of the team members' motivations and how we are delivering gives insights into our culture.

We've made mistakes that you can learn from. For our crucial stakeholders, our team members, our partners and our customers, we still did not do enough with the succession of relationships.

The values constitution helps my successors make decisions. They may not be the decisions I would make, but I have reduced the risk of them being against my values. By building our cultural leadership system, we support the intrinsic motivation of the team while embedding our values constitution. A crucial learning for us was that we could have improved the handover of stakeholder relationships. An example of this is some of our customers. When you found a business like adapt which is delivering a novel offering – a technology-driven service to support SME stewardship – we had a lot of early adopting customers. They had connected to my passion and ideas. The relationship was with me as much as it was with adapt. Being more conscious of this I could have worked harder at the relationship handover.

## Principle 5: Build your Business Way

As you can see, one of our values is to walk the adapt Way. And we have a value that challenges every member of our team to use our offering to build adapt. By having the adapt Way captured with all its forms of data, I was in a good position to support the recruitment and training of an aligned Owner-Leader. The support of the recruitment, induction and training included:

- Supporting the 'data room' that Gabe would use to do his due diligence. The information memorandum was a series of links into the adapt Way data.
- Inducting and training Gabe with speed, given the rapid four months to deploy and assess acumen.
- Providing a succession map to maximise clarity about where we are on the handover of each role.

As an active owner, I have a lot of transparency about the lead indicators of the business, including:

- cultural data
- organisation leadership team health
- team effectiveness data

- strategy (objectives and key results) and progress.
- maps of how we are organised
- visibility of systems.

To make decisions, people want evidence. All my stakeholders wanted evidence and clarity as I traversed the complexity of succession of ownership and leadership. The types of data stored in your Business Way provide important evidence that supports resilience. When I shared my information memorandum with Gabe, I was excited to give him a data-driven tour of our business, with longitudinal evidence as well as sense-making maps.

---

*To make decisions, people want evidence.*

---

## Conclusion

The use of succession thinking from the early stages of ADAPT by Design demonstrates my succession journey.

To be able to hand over roles I needed clarity as to what they were and what teams they impacted. The accountability and acumen required was clear. We could then design the handover plan (see handover plan page 148). I was able to monitor trust in the business as I handed over my roles.

| Team | Role | Note |
|---|---|---|
| Sell | Shared value lead | Gabe as successor |
| Organisation leadership | Team leader (Leader of ADAPT by design) | Gabe as successor |
| Owner-Director | Owner Director | Succession of ownership. Gabe joins as team member. |

My owner vision was documented but it was enriched in searching for my co–Owner-Leader. Gabe and I were co–Owner-Leaders for 18 months so I could support the training associated with the role transitions. To support the alignment and the transition of capital, I added more clarity and detail to my owner vision. Over time, we formed an integrated owners' vision which is now a schedule of our shareholders' agreement. Gabe and I are both referenced as vision custodians in that agreement.

We had been working for some time to build the habits and practices of the organisation leadership team. I was a member of this team. I have now left this team. The induction of Gabe to this team was enhanced by the clarity of the team's habits and practices. Gabe, Jillian, Steve and Dave know I will support them as an elder and in my Owner-Director roles, but I will not reenter this team. Those accountabilities have been handed over. I jokingly say that I've sent in the neuron scrubber so I can't do that work anymore. We determined that, to solve my succession, we had to helicopter in an Owner-Leader. We carefully designed an entry to mitigate as much risk as possible. Part of this risk mitigation was to hand over the technician roles first and make sure Gabe could execute them.

The values were seeded from the beginning. We are all human and we break these values occasionally, however we own them and they're used to guide decision makers. The values were a critical part of the recruitment process and were used extensively to make alignment decisions. The values were critical to the foundation of the business but just as critical to support the succession process.

Having the relevant data available and transparent allowed me to deal with a complex process effectively. All the current team members of ADAPT by Design were well informed about my succession over the 2.5-year period. Everybody involved could get a good understanding of the business because the 'way' data was available. Gabe was ultimately able to do a lot of due diligence around culture, leadership, strategy and systemisation through this data.

Gabe was able to get up and running faster because the sense-making and guidance gave him context. This is true for all new members. Induction and training can be accelerated.

In the next chapter, I will share trends that I think are going to be of great value to Owner-Leaders that are building for the long term.

# Chapter 9
# SUCCESSION THINKING, BUSINESS VALUE AND CAPITAL

## Introduction

The core benefit of applying succession thinking is that you orient the business to deliver to your collective aspirations. The owners' vision focuses on what you want for all the stakeholders of the business. In long-term businesses, the decisions you make about capital will support your vision and also allow you to design solutions that integrate across all your stakeholders.

> *The core benefit of applying succession thinking is that you orient the business to deliver to your collective aspirations.*

You can manage capital by taking loans (using debt capital) or using the shareholding of your business. The following are capital strategies you might consider:

- Integrate leadership and ownership succession (as I did in ADAPT by Design).

- Sell the business wanting great outcomes for the team and the customers.
- Seek investment or debt capital so that you can complete a specific initiative.
- Build an employee-owned company so your succession is the team members.

We will explore each of these options in this chapter. Bear in mind that the way you design and build your business today impacts which of these strategies you can achieve. You may wish to design a succession system where you hand over the vision to aligned stakeholders currently connected to the business. If you sell the business to external parties, they will have a vision of their own. You must be comfortable with handing over control or ensure you agree with their plans.

I will explain how succession thinking enables you to align capital decisions with your vision. This book is about innovating the stewardship of SMEs to deal with challenges and harness the opportunities of an Owner-Leader. I will share information on current trends and capital flows that will impact the stewardship of your SME.

You have a lot of wealth tied up in your business, and future ownership is a core part of your owner vision. You need to integrate getting what you want for the business commercially with what you want for other stakeholders.

In succession thinking, you consider all stakeholders. To make the best decision, you must be clear about your access to capital. What you do with your shareholding is the final succession challenge. In this chapter, we will explore several considerations that will put you in the best position to deal with the debt and equity capital decisions.

In 2007, we – at acQuire – began the work of designing an employee ownership system. Our intention was that shareholding would move from the founding owners to the employees. In 2018, when we sold the business externally, we had 31 employee owners. In many ways this was successful because we'd built a group that owned the culture.

When a person became a shareholder, they would receive a laser-cut block to store the history of their share transactions. Each time they bought shares, they would get a stainless steel rod to put in the block.

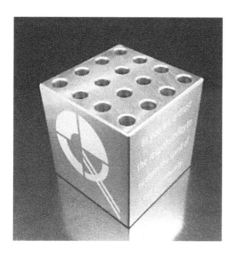

We were building ideas to raise the gravitas of ROV investing, even though we didn't have this term at the time.

We had discovered the interdependence between ownership, leadership and culture. However, there were some major short-comings in our implementation that we never resolved. We did not achieve the succession of ownership to the employees because we couldn't get transition capital at the time the founding owners were keen to hand over. We were prepared to discount the valuation for an internal sale but still could not make that work.

Having the knowledge about ownership succession and its impact on access to capital means you can implement solutions earlier in the life of your business. We put a lot of design work in, but I could not find succession thinking advisers to assist us – hence the foundation of ADAPT by Design and the content of this book.

In this chapter we will explore:

- succession of ownership
- maximising your valuation
- access to capital
- SME stewardship and ESG investing.

## Succession of ownership

When building for the long term, the following questions are important:

- Who will hold the vision custodian accountability?
- Are the capital suppliers investing in your vision or are they intending to change it?

Succession thinking was formed to solve the challenge of building and sustaining SMEs. It is an innovation of SME stewardship designed with the Owner-Leader as the beneficiary. An area still in its infancy is capital and ownership solutions that support long-term stewardship. There are trends associated with people wanting more options to integrate their investing decisions with what they want in the world. Environmental & Social Governance (ESG) investing is one of these.

There is a large opportunity for entrepreneurs who focus specifically on the problem of SME capital. For instance, in the table below I refer to stakeholder ownership, and I have yet to see an implementation where the vision custodianship is part of the design. This is a challenging area to discuss because it's where your business intersects the legal jurisdiction in which you operate. It depends on what type of legal structure you established your business with. We will explore this at a high level, but I will assume you have a limited liability entity – in Australia, we call it a proprietary limited company.

As an SME Owner-Leader, you can put your attention on building your business's capability where the outcome is sustained revenue and profits. Your valuation will be an outcome of that focus. As a succession thinking SME Owner-Leader, you build for the long term and can see the vision realised. Valuations need to be given a lot of thought as part of your succession of ownership strategy. There are many possibilities for business sale, but the following list is typical.

| Ownership succession type | Description | Exit or sustain vision | Opportunity for innovation |
|---|---|---|---|
| *Trade sale* | 100% of shares are sold to a new owner | Exit (exit vision rights) | |
| *Partial sale (investor)* | Usually to raise capital for a specific initiative and the shares are diluted | Sustain (reduce vision rights) | |

| Ownership succession type | Description | Exit or sustain vision | Opportunity for innovation |
|---|---|---|---|
| *IPO* | Initial public offering; float the business on the stock exchange | Exit (reduce vision rights)<br><br>Anyone can participate but now it is ROI | |
| *Employee ownership* | Design a succession system that supports employee ownership | Sustain (reduce vision rights, but can design vision transition) | Significant |
| *Leadership ownership (management buyout)* | In succession thinking this would be a leadership (most likely organisation leaders) buyout | Sustain (reduce vision rights, but can design vision transition) | Significant |
| *Stakeholder ownership* | Owned by nominated stakeholders of the business; for instance employees, customers, partners could all participate in ownership | Sustain (reduce vision rights, but can design vision transition) | Significant |

In the table above, the term 'exit' means to exit vision custodianship, and 'sustain' means that, although augmented, you can sustain vision custodianship.

In addition to this list, there is the potential for more innovation in patient capital. For instance, imagine a patient capital exchange. A place where companies can supply lead indicator data, meet the standards and list. An ROV dividend market. A place where a business can get access to capital without giving up vision control.

In the table above, with ownership frameworks with 'sustain', your vision and values can continue or at least be handed over.

This can be done with an integrated approach to ownership, leadership and culture. When an exit takes place, the owners' vision and the values constitution are fundamentally disrupted.

If you, as a succession thinking Owner-Leader, take a proactive approach to design your succession of ownership solution, you can integrate all that we will discuss in this chapter. The challenge is that many regulatory professionals, namely accountants and lawyers, assist owners to establish shareholder agreements. They ask the owner what they want and it usually gets into a tax optimisation discussion. The owner vision is the starting specification for the design of your succession of ownership model.

Succession of ownership decisions are the biggest and most complex decisions you'll make. Succession thinking puts your business in a good position to execute succession in alignment with your aspirations, as defined in your owner vision. This is the core work of the Owner-Director team.

It was November 2017. My wife Debbie and I spent a lot of time editing a letter that I subsequently sent to my fellow owners and leaders of acQuire. The letter stated that it was time to sell the business. The process gave me gastritis. It was a big decision. The idea of changing the state of my relationship with our people and customers was at the core of my concerns.

However, we proceeded and, in my due diligence for our buyer, I knew our vision was over but I wanted to find a buyer who would let the ship keep sailing as much as possible. We subsequently went through a due diligence process where the team produced 1500 documents in two months. I learned in the process that we were novices at selling businesses. We'd only sold one. The buyers have often done this many times before and you are doing it for the first time.

Our ownership succession was successful because of our succession thinking approach. However, if I was going to do it again, I would have improvements. This is an area I want to help other owners prepare for over time. The sooner you build the capability into the business, the better the outcome will be for you.

This is a large and difficult domain where aspirations meet corporation and tax law. I appreciate the difficulty and recommend working with an adviser (a team member on the Owner-Director team) to do this work. Treat this as a long-term project. Build your knowledge of the problem over time and be patient about the outcome. A trusted adviser who can help support the design is ideal.

## Maximising the value of your business

The more resilience you build into your business, the more you are reducing risks for any potential buyer – this will be valued. If you are going to seek investor capital or are looking to sell your business in the future, it's wise to think about what impacts valuations. The following are common risks associated with the purchase of a business:

- **Financial risks:** Potential buyers will thoroughly examine the financial statements of your business to ensure it has a sound financial foundation.
- **Legal risk:** It's important to review all contracts and legal documents related to your business.
- **Market risk:** Potential buyers will do a thorough analysis of your market and industry to assess the potential risks and opportunities.

- **Operational risk:** This is the risk that the business's operations could fail due to factors such as lack of skilled employees, inadequate systems and processes, or insufficient inventory.
- **Reputational risk:** A business's reputation is a critical asset and any negative publicity or reviews can significantly impact the value of the business.
- **Personnel risk:** When you buy a business you also inherit its employees, and if key employees leave, the business's operations could be severely impacted. It's important to assess employee turnover rate, satisfaction and succession.

However, this does not acknowledge a number of other risks. Owner-Leader risk and a combination of the following can impact a business if the Owner-Leaders have been central to everything and they are no longer participating:

- leadership acumen
- technical and product market knowledge
- customer relationships
- cultural and team member relationships.

It's common for the Owner-Leader to be asked to stay for a period to reduce these risks. This works because, as the previous owner, they are now operating inside a business with a totally different vision and value set. The solutions for these risks need to be found over the lead-up years before the sale, another product of succession thinking.

When you invest in succession thinking, you'll build capability to mitigate these risks. If your aspiration is to build for the long term and then sell your business, you'll drive a higher valuation.

Another important point to make is that life events can happen to anyone. If there is a tragedy in your family, this can have a big impact on your aspirations for the business. Having your business in a form that is ready for sale and being prepared for the due diligence is wise. That is the whole point of this book. When you apply succession thinking, you are ready for anything – including a sale.

You might be thinking that external buyers have other motivations for why a business is valuable to them, like market synergies or product integration. You might also think that they have their own way, so will they value yours? In most cases, they're buying a business they want the people to stay in. If your Business Way can be handed over, this mitigates many relationship risks.

You might struggle to give this any priority now. Let me provide a formula that proves it will take a lot of thinking over a long time. In talking to an Owner-Leader about the sale of her business, she seemed a bit impatient about the work she had to do. I said, 'Can you please tell me about how much effort you put into the last sale you made in your business?' She said, 'Two weeks for a $100,000 order.' I said, 'Give me an approximate figure of how much the business could sell for.' She said, '$5 million.' I said, 'So would it not make sense that you spend 50 ($5 million ÷ $50,000) times two weeks, so 100 weeks, on the sale of your business?' Selling a business is a once-in-a-lifetime decision for many Owner-Leaders so you want to do it as well as possible. Succession thinkers may never want to sell but are always prepared.

---

*Succession thinkers may never want to*
*sell but are always prepared.*

---

## Access to capital

The people that provide capital are taking a risk. The greater the risk, the more expensive the capital and the more onerous the covenants. It is my experience that banks as debt capital suppliers request lag indicator data, data about past financial performance. This makes sense. However, it would make sense to also ask about measurements that are lead indicators of future performance.

I'm going to introduce a sample of what lead indicators are and examine whether this approach could be the ultimate assessment of your business. Like many SME Owner-Leaders, you probably generated reinvestment capital by making profits and keeping your own salary as low as possible. Therefore, your major source of capital is success in the market by serving customers and producing revenue. However, at the start and at different stages, you get capital into your business by borrowing – debt capital – or by selling shares in your business – investor capital or equity. Let's explore your access to these forms of capital:

- **Debt capital:** You must provide security for debt capital – in many cases (including mine), the family home. If you want debt capital during tight financial conditions, be ready to provide a lot of information to the bank. They'll demand lag indicators such as financial statements, which you may find surprising, as I did.

- **Equity capital:** You give an investor a share of your company in return for funds. As we have discussed in succession of ownership, this will be defined by your owners' vision. If you're building for the long term, you are seeking patient investors.

A lender of debt capital, such as a bank, wants to mitigate their risk associated with the loan of capital. You can achieve this by reviewing your capability to service the loan and security on your assets to mitigate as a backstop. An investor of patient capital wants to maximise the probability of dividends. If you can supply the following data, your probability of success of attracting the right partners goes up:

- Leadership:
  - organisation leader capability
  - leadership distribution and fragility
  - stewardship effectiveness:
    - goal and objective setting
    - measurement of progress.
- Culture (team members):
  - employee retention data
  - engagement data
  - employee motivation data
  - team effectiveness data.
- Economic engine performance (beyond financials):
  - pipeline
  - customer loss
  - customer longevity
  - customer revenue concentration
  - business model risk
  - customer and partner relationships.
- Systems:
  - Team organisation – accountability
  - Systems (processes).

When building a business using succession thinking, many of these questions get answered. The items listed are not directly described by the principles, but are the outcomes of effective stewardship. It takes time, but the principals support building a business that has this data. These lead indicators are good measures of future performance.

At the time of writing this book, there was little evidence of new capital offerings that were based on measures of resilience. I know there are opportunities to build new financial products that are designed for the SME patient capital market. However, whether you are looking for debt or investor capital, being able to supply lead indicator data will put you in a good negotiating position.

The following research backs up trends in debt capital. The Ernst & Young report about banking summarises the trends that they see impacting SME banks.[7] Moving beyond traditional segments and data silos will be crucial. Instead of categorising SMEs based on their turnover or number of employees, banks should place greater focus on where they are in their life cycle – from conception to growth, maturity, decline and exit. As part of new segmentation models, getting to the heart of SME behaviours and predicting needs will be crucial. This report and other trends indicate that by building for the long term, you'll be in a good position to harvest these positive banking trends associated with debt capital. By thinking about lead indicators, you'll be in a good negotiating position.

## SME stewardship and ESG investing

Throughout this book, I've argued that by building an SME with succession thinking you could participate in the economy in a

---

7    'The Five-Step Journey to SME Banking Transformation'.

different way. Instead of being the poor cousins of the corporations, we are respected for our excellence of stewardship, capacity to innovate and ability to be agile and resilient.

Succession thinking provides a way to build your SME's stewardship capability so you can deliver sustained value over the long term. Applying succession thinking will make you more attractive to certain types of investors; for example, the environmental, social and governance (ESG) investor. ESG is used to assess an organisation's practices and performance on various sustainability and ethical issues. It also provides a way to measure business risks and opportunities in those areas. In capital markets, some investors use ESG criteria to evaluate companies and help determine their investment plans – a practice known as 'ESG investing'.

The good news for succession thinking Owner-Leaders is you already have the infrastructure. You have the social and governance parts in good shape. All that is left is the environmental part. You can use ESG to enhance your owner vision. It is my opinion that in the near future we will see major growth in the intersection of patient capital and ESG. Your Business Way will be driven by your owner vision. You can provide a transparent and data-driven approach to ESG. Imagine attracting patient capital investors who you know are aligned because you have harnessed the SME advantage. You have the decision rights and size to be an authentic ESG business. You can supply data as proof of your ESG credentials.

Excellence of SME stewardship is a requirement of being able to participate in new forms of capital markets and attract investors. The intersection of ESG and patient capital may be available today, but only on the fringe. This is a growing trend which, as a succession thinker, you can be in a good position to participate in.

You can get in front of these trends and be a leader in the deployment and measurement of ESG. The internal vision construction and considerations for ESG are closely aligned. Succession thinking helps you build the stewardship to deliver.

You might be thinking that this seems a bit futuristic and these concepts seem a little distant from your current business. This may be true, but you are building for the long term. By applying the succession thinking principles, you'll be well set for ESG or other investment and capital trends.

## Conclusion

There are many reasons to build your business for the long term and expand your options as an SME Owner-Leader. Capital is often the constraint to being able to expand into another geography or invest in research and development. You need to build the skills to do this and make sure that, in your desire to obtain capital, you do not derail your owner vision.

The sale of a business is a rare event, and it would be unusual that you are well trained for this. In the past, ownership systems have been established by starting with the legal and tax constraints. Start with your Owners' Vision and then introduce the constraints. Building a good succession-of-ownership framework is a design exercise. This is the work of the Owner-Director team and it takes a lot of thinking and effort.

Stop making decisions about succession of ownership from a purely legal and accounting mindset. Park the car for these big design challenges.

The valuation of your business will be important for any conversation you have with investors. You cannot boost valuation at the 11th hour. It is about having both the track record and the lead indicator data to maximise confidence that the business can continue to be successful. Leaders, lenders and equity investors approach lead indicators in their own way. It's hard to spot a consistent thread. The questions in this chapter are questions that buyers and investors ask. There is a lot of opportunity for disruption in the supply of debt capital to the market.

As a succession thinker, you'll be well set to participate.

# CONCLUSION

You are the silent heroes of our economy who take risks with limited support. The nature of your existence leads to a lonely journey with many challenges. Historically, you've been told that there is one approach to building a business, which is heavily influenced by short-term ROI logic. This does not solve many of your core challenges and you often end up stuck, burned out or not delivering on your aspirations. You have an opportunity to harness the advantages that are not available to large complex businesses with lots of owners. If you realise this, you can have a more energetic and positive view of your business beyond the short-term challenges.

There is a trend where people are searching for purposeful businesses where they can have impact. Harnessing the SME advantages will help you establish a business that is attractive to highly motivated and capable people. As an SME Owner-Leader, if you become a succession thinker and build for the long term, you can lead the charge on making SMEs more valued and visible. You can be one of the frontrunners of building an SME economy founded on ROV.

Succession thinking is a powerful approach for building your business at any stage of its evolution. Unlike succession planning, which is typically used in the latter stages of business, succession thinking focuses on building a strong foundation for long-term value creation. To become a successful succession thinker, it's important to cultivate practices that build trust.

Succession involves handing over decision-making authority for something you deeply care about, which can be challenging. It also requires confronting your own ego and allowing others to thrive in their roles as potential successors. In short, succession thinking is about building a business which can thrive beyond its current Owner-Leaders, and it starts with empowering your team and cultivating trust. By embracing this approach, you can create a business that is built to last and maximise long-term value creation.

Succession thinking is a set of five principles:
- Seek role clarity
- Build your owners' vision
- Build leadership beyond you
- Build culture beyond you
- Build your Business Way.


The roles that are common across SMEs are owner, director, organisation leader, team leader and technician. As an Owner-Leader, you will have a number of these roles and it is common that they are not well defined. It is likely that you are good at some roles and battling in others. Clarity allows you to hand over the ones you don't want or aren't good at.

A common problem in SMEs is the cheetah-eagle problem. People are very good at flying but they want to run. The opposite is also true. Productivity improves when we align wants and capability. Role clarity is central to this outcome. The cheetah–eagle problem is at its greatest with leadership roles – people often have an aspiration to lead without the acumen or the desire to do the necessary learning.

By being mindful of role acumen and how to do role handover, we can increase success in distributing leadership to others. To build a long-term business, you will need to distribute leadership to others. Being clear of types of leadership roles and the acumen to execute them is critical.

Your owner vision is the foundation of building your Business Way, providing guidance for your business and shaping your decision making. It serves as a manifesto for your business, including important areas such as capital decisions, future ownership, growth and compensation. By crafting a clear owner vision, you'll be better equipped to develop effective long-term strategies. For businesses with multiple owners, an integrated owners' vision can help align interests and reduce the risk of unhealthy conflict.

For single owners, having a clearly defined vision is crucial to mitigating risks associated with expanding ownership and identifying areas of non-alignment. Investing time and effort in defining your owner vision is crucial to ensuring your business delivers what you want. Whether your goal is to achieve more discretionary time while growing the business or pursuing other objectives, decision making starts with a clear understanding of your owner vision.

A key to building a business for the long term and being a succession thinker is to invest in leadership. There are two forms of leadership roles that are critical in an SME: the organisation leader and the team leader. The organisation leader is a member of the organisation leadership team. That team has the mandate to deliver the vision.

Developing the skills to do this is in itself a long-term pursuit. Given the nature of an SME, you need to learn on the job and do the shared learning with your teammates. By building a team of leaders who are all responsible for the total business or the total system, you become more antifragile. If any member of the team needs time off or has a life event, the others can lead the business. The business is made up of a set of teams. Each team has a team leader, and that team leader has specific thematic accountabilities as well as general team effectiveness accountabilities.

You may have a need to helicopter leaders into your business for pragmatic reasons. However, getting clarity of your Business Way will assist you to set them up for success in the future. By building the capabilities of team leadership, you can percolate leaders. The first step is for you, as an Owner-Leader, to recognise your role as an organisation leader independent of your other roles.

Building a culture beyond you will build a healthy and highly differentiated workplace. You will create the conditions for distributed decision making because the values constitution will be embedded. This is critical as an Owner-Leader. You can't hand over without being able to trust the system, not just the people. Business culture is a system – it can persist as people change. Your culture needs continuous support and monitoring. With the establishment of cultural leadership, you are putting accountability in place to maintain the culture you want. You are not leaving it to chance.

By developing a team member journey, you can embed your values constitution to support entry, engagement and exit of a team member. A term that has become cliche is to be an employer of choice. You want to build a place that attracts effective and aligned people who can contribute for the long term. Once cultural leadership is established, it can be handed over.

Your Business Way will be maintained by all team members. Your Owner-Director team provides the integrated owners' vision. Your Business Way custodians are the Owner-Director and organisation leadership teams. Its upkeep is by all teams. The data will be there in perpetuity and outlast any specific leader or team member. Your Business Way empowers succession for all in the business. The data will probably exist in a variety of places. Being able to integrate and relate this data is valuable. Your Business Way is made up of interdependent components – a set of guidance, a set of teams, a set of roles related to those teams and a set of team data. All this data can be considered as part of your Business Way.

A well-defined owners' vision will give you greater clarity for making capital decisions. Capital is often the constraint to being able to expand into another geography or invest in research and development. You need to build the skills to make good capital – both debt and equity decisions – and not derail your vision.

Building out your Business Way will assist in building resilience and the capacity to supply lead indicator data. This will have a positive impact on your valuation. Succession thinking is an approach to raise SME stewardship capability and excellence. The trends of ESG and patient capital are worth exploring now. Succession thinking will set you up to harvest these opportunities.

## Common scenarios

The patterns that tend to repeat across SME owners are numerous. You may identify with one or all of the following stories. The three that follow are very common.

## Story 1: Stuck in operations

### *Where you are*

You have each of the following roles, but you don't think about them independently: owner, director, organisation leader, team leader and technician. You usually have multiple technician roles. The work associated with each is aggregated. You may deal with a customer issue followed by a financial issue, then a large strategic decision. Your personal stewardship is marked by being good at getting stuff done, knocking off the transactions as they hit you.

The context switching from a detailed task to a strategy is fatiguing. You tend to be reactive and find it hard to get proactive. You find it hard to get to work on the business and are trapped in operations. You are tired and feel a bit stuck. It is hard to look after engaging the team because you are so busy doing work for the customer. This means that people's issues are growing, and the emotion attached to this is draining.

### *What you want*

You want more discretionary time. You want to get out of operations. You want the business to grow, but without the pressure of boom then bust. You want the business to be financially secure and deliver sustained profits, where markets allow. You want to sustain the business, deal with remuneration and reward you and your fellow owners. You want to be able to take uninterrupted holidays with your family and know the business is solid and in trusted hands. You want to use the discretionary time to do what you want to do on the business. You like working on big thinking and new opportunities.

By being able to do this work, you continue to build a resilient business.

## Story 2: An owner and a principal technician

*Where you are*

You have each of the following roles, but you don't think about them independently: owner, director, organisation leader, team leader and principal technician (maybe an architect or an engineer). You founded your business because you are good at your craft. You identify with your craft and the business has grown around you. You have aspirations that the business lives and you can continue to master your craft. You are a reluctant leader. You have to do organisation leadership and team leadership but don't want to. You think you should be able to do these roles but have never wanted to or been trained for it. However, you have a vision for the business – mostly implicit, not explicit.

*What you want*

Your vision is to continue to deliver excellence in your area of expertise. You want to be an owner, a director and a principal technician, but you don't want to be an organisation leader or a team leader. You want to have discretionary time and work on the big projects you like doing. You want to decrease your workload over the coming years, bit by bit. You want to be an active owner and a vision custodian, so you set up the organisation leaders and team leaders for success. You set up your business for long-term success because you built a contemporary SME that attracts highly capable and aligned craftspeople.

## Story 3: An early stage business

*Where you are*

You don't have roles. You have a wide range of eclectic tasks to get done. You're neither a manager nor a leader, but have all the decision rights for the business. Everyone is in your team, and they also do an eclectic range of tasks that are distributed in the weekly operations meeting. The following roles are not something that you have considered: owner, director, organisation leader, team leader and technician. When your business was only on butcher's paper, you were strategic. You were making something from nothing. Now you have an ever-increasing set of daily tasks.

Your business is still in an early stage. Your culture has been good, but you noticed that it was hard to go from 6 to 12 people. There seem to be a few more inter-team and intra-team issues. You have a healthy runway and you need to increase the size of the team.

### *Where you want to be*

You implemented the succession thinking principles as a means to set the business up and as a platform for growth. By putting in the logic early, you have built your Business Way as the business grew. From an early stage, the business was driven by your aspirations that have been captured in your owner vision. You set yourself up to scale with elegance, not grow with pain.

For those of you who identify with these stories, the application of succession thinking can deliver what you want. For those who don't identify with these, you may still see how the succession thinking principles maximise the probability of delivering on your aspirations.

I've written this book with the intent that you get value by applying the five principles of succession thinking in your business. I've tried to supply enough information so that you can explore these concepts in some depth. You may agree with the core tenet of this book that SME Owner-Leaders need a solution specifically for

SME stewardship. However, you are challenged by where to start, given the daily demands of your business. This is a difficult thing to do without external support, so I recommend searching for a Business Way partner or partners to assist you.

Before executing this search, you need to make a commitment.

If you want to build for the long term – a high-value, resilient business – you need to develop a succession thinking mindset. To consolidate this commitment, you need to allocate some time and funds to the development of your Business Way. By giving it visibility in your financial statements, you make it part of your budgeting and forecasting cycle. You can't *pretend* to build your Business Way – it requires intent in perpetuity.

---

*If you want to build for the long term – a high-value, resilient business – you need to develop a succession thinking mindset.*

---

The starting part is for you to form the Owner-Director team with your fellow owners and to find the accountabilities of that team. One accountability that is on all succession thinking Owner-Director teams is the formation of an integrated owners' vision. It does not matter what SME or what stage of evolution, this is the starting point in the succession thinking. In succession thinking terms, you seek role clarity – owner and director – and then you build your owners' vision.

A core challenge with succession thinking is that you have to lean in to lean out. This means you have to work harder at the beginning to get what you want. Acknowledging this is important. I strongly recommend James Clear's book *Atomic Habits*. This book asserts that to build new habits, there is a method and we need to start small. His laws for building a new habit are to make it obvious, make it attractive, make it easy and make it satisfying. The laws to breaking a habit are the inversion of this. Use these laws to establish a starting succession thinking habit.

## Imagine ...

This Greek proverb sums up succession thinking.

*A society grows great when old people plant trees in whose shade they shall never sit.*

You may have people of a younger generation – children, nieces or nephews – that you care for. You want the world to progress so they live in a healthier society. You have decision rights to build a business that contributes to that healthier society, where leaders can be developed over the long term. A place where leaders invest in succession, and in the success of their successor. Where leaders build the cultures that are both safe and effective workplaces. The business is excellent because of its long-term intent. Your business is conscious of its community and can contribute. Financial investment has changed, and those local community people can direct their superannuation to invest patient capital in your business. They no longer have to use a retail fund which invests in distant international corporations – their funds are supporting local economic growth.

You can now participate in eldership. Your job is not to make decisions, it is to support decision makers. You can contribute to the business until your final breath. The term 'retirement' needs to be redefined because you can contribute in different but important ways. Your business is one of 100,000 operating this way. Society at large and the economy are healthier and more resilient.

The 'too big to fail' problems discovered in the Global Financial Crisis and the COVID crisis will be things of the past. There will still be big entities, but the problem is not what it was.

This may feel a bit utopian, but I think a lot of this is achievable. The following statistics give some indication of where we are today. However, if we focused our attention on this part of the economy, what could the numbers become? To get this attention we need to be great stewards of our business.

| Country | % of population employed in SMEs* | Contribution to GDP | Source |
|---------|-----------------------------------|---------------------|--------|
| Australia | 66% | 57% | Australian Bureau of statistics |
| US | Small businesses are credited with just under two-thirds (63%) of the new jobs created from 1995 to 2021. | 43.5% | https://www.uschamber.com/small-business/state-of-small-business-now |
| EU | 67% (of private sector) | 58% | https://ec.europa.eu/eurostat/web/products-eurostat-news/-/ddn-20200514-1<br><br>https://www.eppgroup.eu/what-we-stand-for/our-priorities/helping-small-business-to-thrive |
| Canada | 88.2% | 53% | https://ised-isde.canada.ca/site/sme-research-statistics/en/key-small-business-statistics/key-small-business-statistics-20221 |
| Malaysia | 66% | 38.3% | https://www.comparehero.my/sme/articles/sme-landscape-malaysia |
| UK | 61% | 51% | https://www.fsb.org.uk/uk-small-business-statistics |
| Global | 50% | 40% | https://www.worldbank.org/en/topic/smefinance |

* **Small and medium-sized enterprises**, abbreviated as SMEs: fewer than 250 persons employed.

SMEs are further subdivided into:

- **micro enterprises**: *fewer than 10* persons employed;
- **small enterprises**: *10 to 49* persons employed;
- **medium-sized enterprises**: *50 to 249* persons employed;
- **Large enterprises**: *250 or more* persons employed.

Imagine if we could raise the SME stewardship capability and then gain access to new patient capital offerings.

I look forward to you joining the succession thinking community to build this resilient SME economy.

# GLOSSARY

## Part A: Generic terms and their context in this book

| Term | Description |
|---|---|
| *Accountability* | A responsibility allocated to a function, team or role that is not time bound. <br><br> *Example:* <br><br> 'Convert opportunities into happy and successful customers.' <br><br> This is a typical accountability for a business development role. |
| *Decision rights* | Provides clarity on which roles in your business can make decisions and what type of decisions. |
| *Governance* | Governance encompasses the system by which an organisation is controlled and operates, and the mechanisms by which it and its people are held to account. Ethics, risk management, compliance and administration are key elements of governance. |
| *Position* | This is a standard term. However, I make it very clear what the difference is between a position and a role. <br><br> In succession thinking, a position refers to a specific job held by an individual with an employment or commercial agreement. A position comprises a set of roles or a role stack the individual executes. The job title reflects the position, not the roles associated with it. |

| Term | Description |
|------|-------------|
| *ROI* | Return on investment. In this case I am refereeing to a short-term ROI mindset. In short-term ROI the return is based on an impatient capital mindset where liquidity of the capital is prioritised. The objective is therefore to maximise the return in a short period of time and the intention of the investment is exactly that. See definition of ROV and its relationship to patient capital. |
| *Role* | A role is a set of accountabilities that can be executed by a person with the required skills and attributes. |
| *SME* | Small to medium enterprise.<br><br>Most definitions relate to head count or total revenue. For instance, in Australia if there are fewer than 250 people in a business it is considered an SME. In Europe it is 400 people.<br><br>My definition of an SME is where there is a big overlap between ownership and leadership. The people working in the business are also the owners of the business. These people have to run their business in a way acceptable to the jurisdiction in which they operate. Through their ownership they can make decisions about the vision for their business. They can then implement strategies and make decisions to deliver their vision. The sum of these decisions can be referred to as decision rights. The people with these decision rights will be called Owner-Leaders. |
| *Stewardship* | Organisational stewardship means seeing a key accountability of your own role is that the business thrives beyond your tenure. You acknowledge that you are accountable to supporting the success of your successors. Within an organisation, stewardship encourages a more cooperative environment focused on group success. This makes sense because it will most likely lead to better outcomes for you as the owner. |
| *Work item or task* | Work to be done that is time bound and specific.<br><br>*Example:*<br><br>Send the proposal to John on Tuesday morning. |

# Part B: Introduced/succession thinking terms

| Term | Description | Why not use a 'standard' term? |
|---|---|---|
| *Role stack* | A set of roles that are grouped to a position. | In SMEs it is typical that each person has a position where they will need to perform a number of roles. Therefore each position has a role stack.<br><br>I needed a term to describe the set of roles that are allocated to a position. |
| *ROV* | Return on vision (relates to short-term ROI as the vision) | Many SME Owner-Leaders have motivations that are more diverse than money. Their aspirations and goals can be captured in a vision. They want to pursue that vision and realise it. A focus on pure short-term ROI will often impact achieving the vision.<br><br>Think of ROV as still including financial success but not at the expense of other important factors. |
| *Your Business Way* | Your Business Way is a set of interdependent data that defines your business and is essential for all subsequent leaders to know. Think of it like a bucket of all the knowledge, wisdom and practices that you think are important for all near future leaders. These will include your owners' vision, your purpose, your values, how you organise yourself and how you differentiate yourself in the market.<br><br>Your Business Way is the baton that is perpetually passed between leaders and supports all in the business with context. | There was no term I could find that describes a set of data that supports the long-term nature of an SME and supports the Owner-Leaders' handover of their business. |

| Term | Description | Why not use a 'standard' term? |
|------|-------------|-------------------------------|
| *Cheetah–Eagle Problem* | Where people have been given a role or seek a role that they do not have the acumen for. Also, where people have a mismatch between aspirations and acumen. | Both animals are equally gifted. There is no hierarchy between them. One is not better than the other one. I introduced this because I could not find an accepted way of discussing the acumen challenge.<br><br>For people who know me, for years I have used the Wedgetail eagle and Wombat problem. The eagle can fly and the wombats are expert burrowers. One of my favourite animals are wombats because they can exist in the desert or the snow – they are adaptable. However, I was told most people think of the eagle as having greater status and that confuses the metaphor. |